L E N A E   B U L T H U I S

My Prayer Diary

Guess What, Jesus?

CRC Publications, GEMS Girls' Clubs

Copublished by CRC Publications, 2850 Kalamazoo Ave. SE, Grand Rapids, MI 49560 and GEMS Girls' Clubs, 1333 Alger SE, Grand Rapids, MI 49510.

We welcome your comments. Call 1-800-333-8300 or e-mail us at editors@crcpublications.org.

Library of Congress Cataloging-in-Publication Data

Bulthuis, Lenae, 1968-
      Guess what, Jesus? : my prayer diary /
Lenae Bulthuis.
          p.   cm.
      Summary: A devotional prayer journal with daily scripture readings and activities for each day of twelve weeks.
      ISBN 1-56212-475-7
      1. Girls Prayer-books and devotions—English. [1. Prayer books and devotions.] I. Title.
BV4860.B85   1999
242'.62—dc21
                                                                99-29531
                                                                CIP

10 9 8 7 6 5 4 3 2 1

To my husband, Michael Bulthuis. Thank you for your love and listening ear. Your frequent grocery trips, delicious meals, and labor in the laundry room were key to meeting deadlines. I love you.

To my three daughters, Elizabeth, Stephanie, and Melanie Bulthuis. These devotionals were written for you! Dad and I love you dearly and pray without ceasing that your faith and prayer life will grow stronger with each new day.

To my best friend, Diane Zuidema. This book was penned because of your time investment, invaluable critiques, and shared dreams. A heartfelt thanks for your firm belief that this dream would become reality.

Contents

Preface

Jesus has been the number one love in my life since I was a small girl. I learned about him through my dad and mom, my church, and the Christian education I received at school.

Although I grew up reading the Bible and praying every day, it wasn't until I was twenty-six years old that I discovered the power of prayer through journaling. It changed my life!

Instead of whispering a few lines to God before I go to sleep, I write my prayers in a journal. I focus on the four parts of prayer—praise, confession, asking, and thanksgiving. My prayers get dated twice—the day I write my prayers and the day God answers my prayers.

I am filled with joy that God changed my life through prayer, but I have a few regrets. I regret that I didn't find the power of prayer when I was younger. I regret that I didn't experience the adventure of prayer when I was a young girl.

Although I can't go back in time, I can look forward. I hope to help girls—I hope to help *you*—change your life through prayer while you are still young.

Would you like to begin a prayer adventure? If you do, *Guess What, Jesus?* is for you. If you don't know Jesus and his love for you, this book will tell you how to begin a life-long relationship with him. If you do know him as your Savior, *Guess What, Jesus?* will change your prayer life.

Begin today! Journal your prayers. Read your Bible. Use this book as a treasured tool in building your relationship with Jesus.

My prayer for each girl who uses *Guess What, Jesus?* for her prayer diary is this: May your life be changed through prayer, may your love for Jesus grow, and may you have no regrets!

■ Theme for the Week: Prayer

■ Key Verse for the Week

Do not be anxious about anything, but in everything, by prayer and petition, with thanksgiving, present your requests to God.
—Philippians 4:6

■ Bible Reading: Philippians 4:6-7

Warning: Changed Life Ahead!

Get ready, get set, go! Your life will not be the same after you start your adventure of prayer and Bible reading. You don't have to wait until you're old enough, pretty enough, or smart enough. You can begin your adventure today!

God's Word tells you how to begin your journey. Philippians 4:6 says, "But in everything, by prayer and petition, with thanksgiving, present your requests to God."

Prayer is a special time when you talk to God, who listens to each and every word you say. You can talk to God anytime, any-where, and about anything. When you pray, you can

- *praise* God for being your Father in heaven
- *confess* the things you've done wrong
- *ask* God to help you and others
- *thank* God for listening to your prayers

You are God's very special daughter. God wants to hear from you! You'll be blessed by God as you begin your journey of prayer and Bible reading.

■ Something to Think About

Warning! Your prayer time will change your life—and the lives of those around you! When you tell others about the awesome time you're having with God each day, they're going to want to pray more too.

Dear Jesus,

I praise you for _____

_____

_____

I'm sorry for _____

_____

_____

I ask you for _____

_____

_____

I thank you for _____

_____

_____ Amen.

Use markers, highlighters, glitter crayons, colored pencils, and so on to color the theme word for this week. Have fun!

PRAYER

■ **Theme for the Week: Prayer**

■ **Key Verse for the Week**

Do not be anxious about anything, but in everything, by prayer and petition, with thanksgiving, present your requests to God.
—*Philippians 4:6*

■ **Bible Reading: James 5:13-16**

Call Your Prayer Line

We can find many reasons for praying in today's Bible reading from James 5. God wants you to pray when you're happy, when you're in trouble, when you're sick, or when you've sinned.

Many people only pray when they're in trouble. Have you ever been stuck on a math problem and prayed a quick, "Help, Lord! I don't get it!" Or maybe you've asked God to help you find a good time to tell your mom you broke her favorite dish. It's OK to pray when you're in trouble, but that's not the only time God wants you to use your prayer line.

God wants to hear about each part of your day. Tell God what made you happy or sad today. Ask God to make a friend feel well again. Praise and thank God for the special blessings you've experienced today. God cares and listens to each part of your prayers.

■ **Something to Think About**

Has someone in your family ever told you to get off the phone because you've been talking too long? God will never ask you to be quiet because you've been praying too long. God loves to hear from you any time of the day or night. In fact, God gives you a twenty-four-hour, seven-day-a-week prayer line to heaven each and every day forever. And you'll never get a busy signal. Make a call now!

Dear Jesus,

I praise you for _____

_____

I'm sorry for _____

_____

I ask you for _____

_____

I thank you for _____

_____ Amen.

Prayer Word Search

Find ten times when you can pray in this puzzle!

I can pray when I'm . . .

AFRAID   HAPPY
ANGRY   JOYFUL
CHEERFUL   LAUGHING
EXCITED   SAD
GLAD   SMILING

S	L	E	X	C	I	T	E	D
A	A	U	U	G	J	F	L	J
F	H	D	F	U	J	A	R	O
R	A	G	N	R	U	N	O	Y
A	P	K	J	G	E	W	Q	F
I	P	R	H	G	U	E	Z	U
D	Y	I	L	V	T	S	H	L
U	N	A	Y	R	G	N	A	C
G	D	S	M	I	L	I	N	G

■ Theme for the Week: Prayer

■ Key Verse for the Week

Do not be anxious about anything, but in everything, by prayer and petition, with thanksgiving, present your requests to God.
—Philippians 4:6

■ Bible Reading: Luke 11:1-4

The Lord's Prayer

Don't be embarrassed if you've ever thought or said, "I don't know how to pray." Many people feel this way. Even Jesus' disciples weren't sure how to pray, and they asked Jesus to teach them.

Here is the prayer Jesus taught his disciples (you can find it in Luke 11:24):

Praise: *Father, hallowed be your name, your kingdom come.*

Asking: *Give us each day our daily bread.*

Confession: *Forgive us our sins, for we also forgive everyone who sins against us. And lead us not into temptation.*

Thanks: *Always end your prayers by thanking God. You can thank God for taking care of you, for listening to your prayers, and for forgiving your sins.*

We call this prayer the Lord's Prayer. God loves to hear you pray it too. Each time you pray the Lord's Prayer, think about the words and pray it from your heart.

■ Something to Think About

Ask your family to say the Lord's Prayer together before your next meal. Share with them what you learned today about this special prayer.

Dear Jesus,

I praise you for _____

_____

_____

I'm sorry for _____

_____

_____

I ask you for _____

_____

_____

I thank you for _____

_____

_____ *Amen.*

Grid Drawing

To learn how to pray, we need to follow Jesus' example. To learn how to draw praying hands, follow the example on the left. You need a pencil, an eraser, and lots of patience!

■ Theme for the Week: Prayer

■ Key Versc for the Week

Do not be anxious about anything, but in everything, by prayer and petition, with thanksgiving, present your requests to God.
—*Philippians 4:6*

■ Bible Reading: Matthew 6:5-6

Prayer Closets

Where are you sitting right now? When you have your prayer and Bible reading time, do you sit at the kitchen table or in another busy room where the whole family can see what you're doing? Or do you go into your room, shut the door, and spend time alone with God?

In Matthew 6:6 Jesus says, "But when you pray, go into your room, close the door and pray to your Father, who is unseen." When you're in church or having devotions, you're praying with other people. Personal devotions are different, though. That's the time you and Jesus spend together, just the two of you.

Where can you go to be alone with Jesus as you pray and read your Bible? Being alone with Jesus is kind of hard when you share your bedroom and don't have a space to call your own. So ask your mom or dad to help you find a prayer closet for your personal devotions. It doesn't matter if it's a room, a real closet, a corner in the attic, or the back of the garage.

■ Something to Think About

Jonah probably had the most unique prayer closet of anyone in history. For three days and three nights Jonah found himself praying inside the belly of a whale. It's true! You can read Jonah's story in Jonah 1 and 2.

Dear Jesus,

I praise you for _____

_____

_____

I'm sorry for _____

_____

_____

I ask you for _____

_____

_____

I thank you for _____

_____

_____ Amen.

Crack the Code!

Just crack the code and remember to do what Jesus said.

$\overline{\iota}\ \overline{\nu}\quad \overline{\alpha}\quad \overline{\theta}\ \overline{\upsilon}\ \overline{\iota}\ \overline{\epsilon}\ \overline{\tau}\quad \overline{\chi}\ \overline{\lambda}\ \overline{o}\ \overline{\sigma}\ \overline{\epsilon}\ \overline{\tau}\quad \overline{\epsilon}\ \overline{\varpi}\ \overline{\epsilon}\ \overline{\rho}\ \overline{\psi}\quad \overline{\delta}\ \overline{\alpha}\ \overline{\psi}'$

$\overline{\tau}\ \overline{o}\quad \overline{\mu}\ \overline{\psi}\quad \overline{\phi}\ \overline{\alpha}\ \overline{\tau}\ \overline{\eta}\ \overline{\epsilon}\ \overline{\rho}\quad \overline{\iota}\quad \overline{\omega}\ \overline{\iota}\ \overline{\lambda}\ \overline{\lambda}\quad \overline{\pi}\ \overline{\rho}\ \overline{\alpha}\ \overline{\psi}.$

Key					
	A = α	**F** = φ	**M** = μ	**Q** = θ	**U** = υ
	C = χ	**H** = η	**N** = ν	**R** = ρ	**V** = ϖ
	D = δ	**I** = ι	**O** = o	**S** = σ	**W** = ω
	E = ε	**L** = λ	**P** = π	**T** = τ	**Y** = ψ

■ Theme for the Week: Prayer

■ Key Verse for the Week

Do not be anxious about anything, but in everything, by prayer and petition, with thanksgiving, present your requests to God.
—Philippians 4:6

■ Bible Reading: Daniel 6:6-23

Lion Lunch Meat?

Daniel never missed his prayer time, even when it meant he'd be thrown into a den of hungry lions—the kings of the beasts. Daniel decided he'd rather be the lions' lunch than miss his prayer time.

King Darius couldn't save Daniel from the lions, but our great God—the King of kings—could! God shut the mouths of the lions, and Daniel was pulled out of the den the next morning without a single scratch or tooth mark.

Do you always remember to have your Bible reading and prayer time with God every day? If you're like most people, you sometimes stay up late and feel too tired to pray. Or maybe you start watching a movie and forget all about your personal devotions. Although God misses your quiet time together when those things happen, he's always ready to pick up where you left off.

Ask God to help you remember your prayer time every day. And don't forget to thank God that you can pray without worrying about those hungry lions!

■ Something to Think About

If you didn't take the time to read today's Bible passage, read it now. It's an amazing story, and every word is true. What would you have done if you had been in Daniel's shoes? Are there times and places when you find it hard to pray?

Dear Jesus,

I praise you for _____

_____

_____

I'm sorry for _____

_____

_____

I ask you for _____

_____

_____

I thank you for _____

_____

_____ Amen.

Never Forget Notepad

What You Need

4" x 6" (10 cm x 15 cm) rectangle of cardboard or posterboard
2" x 3" (5 cm x 8 cm) notepad
Pencil
Glue
Markers, glitter crayons, stickers, or rubber stamps and ink pad
Yarn or string

How to Do It

1. Glue the notepad in the center of the rectangle of cardboard or tagboard.
2. Decorate the frame around the notepad with markers, glitter crayons, stickers, or rubber-stamp designs.
3. Tie yarn or string around the pencil eraser, and tape one end to the back of the prayer reminder pad.
4. Tape a yarn hanger to the top corners of the prayer reminder pad, and hang it by your prayer closet.
5. Write things you want to pray about on your reminder pad.

■ Theme for the Week: Prayer

■ Key Verse for the Week

Do not be anxious about anything, but in everything, by prayer and petition, with thanksgiving, present your requests to God.
—*Philippians 4:6*

■ Bible Reading: Matthew 6:7-8

Empty Prayers and Water Glasses

Before breakfast, have you ever prayed, *Now I lay me down to sleep. I pray the Lord my soul to keep?* Or maybe you've started your bedtime prayer by saying, *God is great. God is good. Thank you for this food. Amen.*

When people pray without thinking about what they're saying or who they're talking to, their prayers are empty or meaningless. These prayers are as useless to God as an empty water glass is to a thirsty runner.

Jesus warned about empty prayers in Matthew 6:7: "And when you pray, do not keep on babbling like pagans, for they think they will be heard because of their many words."

So don't try to impress God or others with your fancy words or lengthy prayers. When you pray, think about the words you are saying. And when you are writing in your prayer diary, don't worry about misspelled words, where to place the periods and commas, or neat penmanship. God cares about the things that are in your heart.

Let your prayers reflect your real thoughts and feelings. God wants prayers that are sincere. Those are the prayers that come straight from your heart!

■ Something to Think About

Aren't you glad that God doesn't take out a red pen and correct your grammar or spelling when you write in your prayer diary? The only words and phrases that God doesn't like are ones that are empty and meaningless!

Dear Jesus,

I praise you for _____
_____
_____

I'm sorry for _____
_____
_____

I ask you for _____
_____
_____

I thank you for _____
_____
_____ *Amen.*

Orange Julius

Empty prayers are as useless to God as an empty glass is when you're thirsty! The next time your mouth is watering for a cold, delicious drink, make yourself (and your family) an Orange Julius.

What You Need
1 6 oz. (180 mL) can frozen orange juice
½ cup (.12 L) sugar
1 cup (.24 L) cold water
1 cup (.24 L) milk
1 teaspoon (5 mL) vanilla extract
10 ice cubes
Blender

How to Do It
1. Ask an adult for permission to work in the kitchen.
2. Put the first five ingredients in the blender.
3. Process the mixture at high speed.
4. Add the ice cubes.
5. Blend until smooth and serve immediately.

■ **Theme for the Week: Prayer**

■ **Key Verse for the Week**

Write the key verse for the week on the lines below.

_____

_____

_____

_____

—*Philippians 4:6*

■ **This Week I Learned . . .**

Sunday

Prayer is talking to God. My prayer time will change my life forever (Philippians 4:6-7).

Monday

God wants to hear my prayers all the time, not just when I'm in trouble (James 5:13-16).

Tuesday

Jesus taught his disciples how to pray using the Lord's Prayer. I can pray this prayer too (Luke 11:1-4).

Wednesday

I need a quiet place to be alone with Jesus when I pray and read my Bible (Matthew 6:5-6).

Thursday

Prayer should be just as important to me as it was to Daniel (Daniel 6:6-23).

Friday

God wants prayers that come straight from my heart, not empty words (Matthew 6:7-8).

■ **Something to Think About**

Has your prayer life changed this week? What is different about it?

_____

_____

Dear Jesus,

I praise you for _____

_____

_____

I'm sorry for _____

_____

_____

I ask you for _____

_____

_____

I thank you for _____

_____

_____ Amen.

Invisible Prayer Messages

Write invisible messages to your family and friends to tell them that you've been praying for them and that you love them. Be sure to tell them how to make the message appear!

What You Need
Paintbrush
Lemon juice
White paper
Envelopes

How to Do It
1. Dip the paintbrush in lemon juice.
2. Write your secret message on the white paper. Allow the juice to dry.
3. Tell your family and friends to hold the message next to a hot light bulb to read it. (You might want to write this on the envelope.)

■ Theme for the Week: Praise

■ Key Verse for the Week

Let them praise the name of the LORD, for his name alone is exalted; his splendor is above the earth and the heavens.

—Psalm 148:13

■ Bible Reading: Psalm 148

Join the Choir

Have you ever heard the sounds of sea creatures, stormy winds, or cattle? According to Psalm 148, all those sounds together make up the choir that sings God's praises. You won't find their music in your favorite bookstore, though.

To discover one of the most unique choirs you'll ever hear, read Psalm 148 again. Can you find ten choir members listed in the psalm? We've started you off with one example.

1. Lightning and hail
2. _____
3. _____
4. _____
5. _____
6. _____
7. _____
8. _____
9. _____
10. _____

Only God, our almighty creator, deserves the kind of praise this psalm describes. God wants you to listen to this awesome choir. Better yet, God wants you to join the choir. If you don't believe it, read verse 12 again: "Young maidens and children," praise God! This means you!

■ Something to Think About

You can join the praise choir today. Add these words to the psalm (write your name in the blank):

Praise the Lord, _____ !
Praise the Lord!

Guess What, Jesus?

Dear Jesus,

I praise you for _____

_____

_____

I'm sorry for _____

_____

_____

I ask you for _____

_____

_____

I thank you for _____

_____

_____ Amen.

Pet Rock

What You Need

Rocks and pebbles
Tempera paint (optional)
Brush (optional)
Tacky glue
Two wiggly eyes

How to Do It

1. Find a rock for the body and four pebbles to use for ears and feet. If you wish, paint the rock and pebbles with tempera paint.
2. Experiment with the pebbles and rock to create the look you want, and then glue the pebble ears and feet in place.
3. Glue wiggly eyes on the rock.
4. Set your pet rock in a special place to remind you that all creation sings praises to God. You can too!

■ Theme for the Week: Praise

■ Key Verse for the Week

Let them praise the name of the LORD, for his name alone is exalted; his splendor is above the earth and the heavens.

—Psalm 148:13

■ Bible Reading: Psalm 33:1-3; Psalm 40:3

Are Your Mouth and Heart Singing the Same Song?

The Lord loves to hear you sing and make music. Whether you're singing in the bathtub, practicing a hymn on the piano, or whistling your favorite praise song, God is praised. Did you know that there's a special way God always wants you to sing?

Psalm 33:1 tells us about that special way: "Sing joyfully to the LORD, you righteous; it is fitting for the upright to praise him." God wants you to sing with *joy!*

There will be times when you aren't feeling joyful. If you've just had a quarrel with your best friend, if your dog runs away and you can't find him, or if someone you love is sick, it's hard to feel the kind of joy the psalmist is singing about. God knows this, and God cares about your hurts and sadness. It's OK to express those feelings too.

But if you sing "I've got the joy, joy, joy, joy down in my heart" with a frown on your face, people will have a hard time believing that you really mean what you're singing. And you won't feel like you're praising God either. Jesus is listening for your mouth and heart to sing the same song. So when you're praising God, shout your praises *joyfully!*

■ Something to Think About

The next time you sing praises to God, smile until your cheek muscles hurt. Let the joy in your heart escape through your smile!

Dear Jesus,

I praise you for _____

_____

_____

I'm sorry for _____

_____

_____

I ask you for _____

_____

_____

I thank you for _____

_____

_____ *Amen.*

Top Five Favorites

Page through one of your praise songbooks or your church hymnbook and look for songs that praise the Lord. Write the titles of your five favorites below.

1. _____

2. _____

3. _____

4. _____

5. _____

W E E K 2 T W O T U E S D A Y _____

■ Theme for the Week: Praise

■ Key Verse for the Week

Let them praise the name of the LORD, for his name alone is exalted; his splendor is above the earth and the heavens.

—Psalm 148:13

■ Bible Reading: Psalm 105:1-5

Wow! You're Good at That!

What do you do that your family and friends say, "Wow! You're good at that!" Is it singing, playing softball, reading, drawing, caring for pets, listening? Think of three things that you're good at and write them on the lines below.

1. _____
2. _____
3. _____

Each of us is good at a lot of things, but our God is good at *everything!* God loves to hear his daughters and sons praise him by telling the things God has done for them. Praise God now by listing three things God is good at. *Hint:* Think of things God has made, the way God takes care of you, God's great love . . . the list could go on forever.

1. _____
2. _____
3. _____

■ Something to Think About

During your prayer time, praise God for the wonderful things he does for you. Use the three things you wrote down, and add them to your prayer journal too. How long do you think it would take to list all the things God is good at?

Dear Jesus,

I praise you for _____

_____

_____

I'm sorry for _____

_____

_____

I ask you for _____

_____

_____

I thank you for _____

_____

_____ *Amen.*

Day Brightener

Can you think of a family member or a friend who is really good at something? Maybe you know someone who's a great soccer player or bakes the best chocolate chip cookies you've ever tasted or is always smiling and making people feel happy. Maybe she just won a coloring contest.

- Who are you thinking about? _____
- What is this person good at? _____

Tell this person *today* what a good job she or he is doing. You can send a card or an e-mail message, use the telephone, or talk face-to-face. You'll make that person's day very special, and you'll feel good about building someone up with praise!

■ **Theme for the Week: Praise**

■ **Key Verse for the Week**

Let them praise the name of the LORD, for his name alone is exalted; his splendor is above the earth and the heavens.

—*Psalm 148:13*

■ **Bible Reading: Psalm 92:1-3; Psalm 34:1**

Praise the Lord—for a Bad Hair Day?

Have you ever woken up on the wrong side of the bed? Maybe it was one of those mornings when you accidentally dropped your toothbrush in the toilet or poured orange juice on your Cheerios. On a morning like that, did you feel like praising the Lord?

Most people don't feel like praising the Lord when they're having a bad day. But Psalm 34:1 says, "I will extol the Lord at all times; his praise will always be on my lips." Praising the Lord morning, noon, and night is easy to do when everything is going right. When things go from bad to worse, though, it's hard to keep praising the Lord.

We can do it because God's goodness to us is always bigger than the things that bother us. The joy God gives us will always outlast our hurts.

Being the kind of person who can praise the Lord every day in all things takes prayer and practice. Ask the Lord to help you to remember to praise God day and night. Practice praising God in all things.

The next time something bad happens, think of one good thing you can praise God for. Even if you're having a bad hair day, you can still praise the Lord, who knows exactly how many hairs are on your head!

■ **Something to Think About**

Need a little praise reminder now and then? Write "Praise the Lord" on two scraps of colorful paper or sticky notes. Put one by your toothbrush and one on your pillow. When you brush your teeth in the morning, give praise for who God is. When you go to bed at night, give praise for something God did for you.

Dear Jesus,

I praise you for _____

_____

_____

I'm sorry for _____

_____

_____

I ask you for _____

_____

_____

I thank you for _____

_____

_____ Amen.

Praise Maze
This maze will help you remember to praise the Lord from morning to night. Start at the sun and end at the moon!

START

FINISH

■ Theme for the Week: Praise

■ Key Verse for the Week

Let them praise the name of the LORD, for his name alone is exalted; his splendor is above the earth and the heavens.
—*Psalm 148:13.*

■ Bible Reading: 1 Peter 4:7-11

Praise God After the Amen!

It's important to praise God during your prayer time, but does your praise time stop for the day when you end your prayer with the Amen? Today's Bible reading tells us it shouldn't. You can praise God when you love, forgive, serve, speak, or use any of the special talents God has given you.

First Peter 4:11 says, "In all things God may be praised through Jesus Christ. To him be the glory and the power for ever and ever. Amen." You can praise God *in all things*— when you're taking a spelling test, helping a friend, playing a game, writing a letter, or cleaning your room!

When your mom tells you it's time to clean your room, how can you praise God? Do you

___ grumble and complain and leave it messy?

___ clean it cheerfully and do your very best?

___ hide everything under the bed to make it look clean?

If you want to praise God after the Amen, clean your room cheerfully! (And chase a few dust bunnies out from under the bed!)

■ Something to Think About

After you end your prayer today with Amen, how are you going to praise God? Write down one way, and then do it!

Dear Jesus,

I praise you for _____

_____

_____

I'm sorry for _____

_____

_____

I ask you for _____

_____

_____

I thank you for _____

_____

_____ Amen.

PTL (Praise the Lord) Word Search

Find fifteen ways you can praise the Lord in this puzzle.

I can praise God when I . . .

PLAY   HELP
SERVE   LAUGH
BABYSIT   OBEY
CLEAN   DRAW
BIKE   EAT
SING   PRAY
WORSHIP   SHARE

P	L	A	Y	U	D	Y	C	Y	N	T
N	S	K	W	A	L	K	P	R	C	E
Y	E	B	O	K	G	R	R	E	L	T
R	R	A	R	J	N	E	A	I	E	A
I	V	H	T	T	I	S	Y	B	A	B
T	E	O	G	I	S	S	R	Y	N	I
E	W	N	S	A	L	P	Y	D	A	K
W	O	R	S	H	I	P	E	R	A	E
S	U	H	L	E	A	K	R	A	L	D
H	G	U	A	L	U	R	I	W	L	P
K	H	W	A	P	C	H	E	P	W	S

■ Theme for the Week: Praise

■ Key Verse for the Week

Let them praise the name of the LORD, for his name alone is exalted; his splendor is above the earth and the heavens.

—*Psalm 148:13*

■ Bible Reading: 1 Chronicles 16:23-25

Be a Praise Leader for God!

Have you ever seen cheerleaders or fans who are fanatic about their team? During the games they dress in their team's colors, make banners that say "Go! Fight! Win!" and cheer so loudly their throats hurt.

Praise leaders are different than cheerleaders. Praise leaders don't wear a certain color uniform or carry around "Praise the Lord" banners or shout, "God's #1!" as they walk down the halls.

So just what does a praise leader do? Look at these words from 1 Chronicles 16:24: "Declare his glory among the nations, his marvelous deeds among all peoples."

God wants you to be a praise leader too! You can start today by filling in the blanks in the praise sentence below. In the first blank fill in the name of a place (here are some examples to get you started: home, school, church, playground). In the second blank, list a marvelous deed God has done for you (like dying on the cross, making animals, giving you a loving family).

Declare his glory at _____, his _____ among all peoples.

■ Something to Think About

Read your praise leader sentence to a friend or someone in your family. Invite him or her to become a praise leader too by filling in the blanks with their own words. Praise God together!

Dear Jesus,

I praise you for _____
_____
_____

I'm sorry for _____
_____
_____

I ask you for _____
_____
_____

I thank you for _____
_____
_____ *Amen.*

Praise Banner

Make a praise banner for your bedroom to help you remember to praise the Lord!

What You Need

Large sheet of construction paper, posterboard, or freezer wrap

Pencil

Crayons, markers, or paints

Stickers or other decorative materials

How to Do It

1. Use a large sheet of construction paper, or cut posterboard or freezer wrap the size you want your banner.
2. Use a pencil to write a praise sentence on the banner or copy a praise verse from the Bible. (Pick a favorite praise verse from the psalms you've been reading this week.)
3. Use crayons, markers, or paints to color the letters and add designs. Or add stickers or other decorative trims. Be creative!

■ Theme for the Week: Praise

■ Key Verse for the Week

Write the key verse for the week on the lines below.

_____

_____

_____

_____

—*Psalm 148:13*

■ This Week I Learned . . .

Sunday
God wants everything and everyone to praise him. God deserves my praise (Psalm 148).

Monday
My mouth and my heart need to sing the same praise songs (Psalm 33:1-3; Psalm 40:3).

Tuesday
God is good at everything! I can praise God for all the wonderful things he has done for me (Psalm 105:1-5).

Wednesday
I can praise God every day—morning, noon, and night—even on bad days (Psalm 92:1-3; Psalm 34:1).

Thursday
I can praise God when I pray and in everything I do (1 Peter 4:7-11).

Friday
I can be a praise leader by telling others about the wonderful things God has done (1 Chronicles 16:23-25).

■ Something to Think About

How did you praise God this week?

_____

_____

_____

_____

Dear Jesus,

I praise you for _____

_____

_____

I'm sorry for _____

_____

_____

I ask you for _____

_____

_____

I thank you for _____

_____

_____ Amen.

PTL (Praise the Lord) Tambourine

Make this rhythm instrument and shake it when you sing your favorite praise songs.

What You Need

Two aluminum foil pie plates
Handful of small pebbles or dried beans
Stapler
Stickers or ribbon (optional)

How to Do It

1. Put a handful of small pebbles or dried beans in one of the aluminum pie plates.
2. Place the second pie plate over the first one and staple the rims together.
3. If you wish, decorate the tambourine with stickers or ribbon streamers.

■ Theme for the Week: Confession

■ Key Verse for the Week

Forgive us our sins, for we also forgive every-one who sins against us.

—*Luke 11:4*

■ Bible Reading: Luke 11:1-4

Tiny Teardrops and Deep Oceans

Have you ever had to confess to your dad that you were the one who forgot to feed the dog? Or have you ever needed to confess to your teacher that you cheated on a homework assignment? You're not alone. Everyone sins.

Jesus taught his disciples—and you and me—to confess our sins when we pray. Confession means telling God your sins and then asking God to forgive you. Forgiveness has two parts. Luke 11:4 says, "Forgive us our sins." Ask God for it in your prayers. That's the first part.

Luke 11:4 also says, "for we also forgive everyone who sins against us." Forgiving others as Jesus forgives us is the second part.

If you listed all the bad things other people have done to you and then listed all the bad things you've done to hurt Jesus, which list would be longer? When you forgive others, it's like blinking away a tiny teardrop full of sins. When Jesus forgives you, it's like washing away a deep ocean full of sins. If Jesus can forgive an ocean full of sins, then follow his example and always be ready to forgive other people for their teardrops of sins.

■ Something to Think About

During your prayer time today, think about the two parts of forgiveness. What sins do you need to ask God to forgive? Do you need to forgive someone else?

Dear Jesus,

I praise you for _____

_____

_____

I'm sorry for _____

_____

_____

I ask you for _____

_____

_____

I thank you for _____

_____

_____ Amen.

Use markers, highlighters, glitter crayons, colored pencils, and so on to color the theme word for this week. Be creative!

CONFESSION

■ Theme for the Week: Confession

■ Key Verse for the Week

Forgive us our sins, for we also forgive everyone who sins against us.
—Luke 11:4

■ Bible Reading: Isaiah 55:6-7

It's Free!

Are you saving money to buy something special? One of the first questions you probably asked when you started saving your hard-earned dollars is, How much will it cost?

The best gift you will ever receive, though, isn't for sale. You don't need to buy it because it's free! God's gift to you is Jesus. Do you want to know how much this gift costs? It is very, very expensive. It cost Jesus his life.

God loved you so much that he gave Jesus to die for your sins. Three days later, Jesus rose again from the dead. When Jesus died and came back to life, he paid the price for your sins and mine.

But how much does God's gift cost *you?* It's free! Isaiah 55:7 says, "Let him turn to the LORD, and he will have mercy on him, and to our God, for he will freely pardon."

In order to pay for your sins, you don't have to do a hundred good things for your family or put lots of money in the offering plate each week. There's no cost for forgiveness. It's yours for the asking!

■ Something to Think About

There's only one way to be forgiven. You have to repent and be sorry for your sins! The best news is that God will freely forgive us. So remember to ask God for forgiveness today.

Dear Jesus,

I praise you for _____

_____

_____

I'm sorry for _____

_____

_____

I ask you for _____

_____

_____

I thank you for _____

_____

_____ Amen.

Math Game

_____	How many Psalms are in the Bible?
+ _____	How many disciples did Jesus have? (Mark 3:14)
+ _____	How many books are in the Old Testament?
− _____	How old was Abraham when he died? (Genesis 25:7)
+ _____	How many days did it rain on Noah's ark? (Genesis 7:4)
+ _____	How many chapters are in the book of 2 Timothy?
− _____	How many commandments did God gives Moses? (Exodus 20)
+ _____	On what day did God make man and woman? (Genesis 1:27, 31)
− _____	How many books are in the Bible?
(Total) _____	How much will it cost you to receive God's forgiveness?

Your total is the price that you must pay for God's forgiveness.
(If your answer isn't zero, grab a calculator and try again!)

■ Theme for the Week: Confession

■ Key Verse for the Week

Forgive us our sins, for we also forgive every-one who sins against us.
— *Luke 11:4*

■ Bible Reading: Psalm 51:16-17

Going Through the Motions

Have you ever said "I'm sorry" to someone and not meant it? Maybe your mom made you apologize to your cousin for losing her favorite necklace. Maybe your mom even made you apologize *two* times because it didn't sound like you really meant it the first time.

When you say you're sorry even when you really aren't, it's called "going through the motions." Some people in the Old Testament offered sacrifices to God to show they were sorry for their sins. The only problem was they were only going through the motions. They didn't really mean it. Psalm 51:16 tells us that God does "not delight in sacrifice" like this.

What God wants to see when you ask for forgiveness is "a broken and contrite heart" (Psalm 51:17). A broken heart doesn't need a doctor to fix it. A broken heart is a heart that's sad and sorry for the wrong things you've done to hurt God and others.

So don't just go through the motions. God knows if you really mean it when you say, "I'm sorry." God doesn't just listen to your words. He's looking for a broken heart.

■ Something to Think About

If your heart is broken because you're truly sorry for your sins, here's great news! God can fix your broken heart and forgive your sins.

Dear Jesus,

I praise you for _____

_____

_____

I'm sorry for _____

_____

_____

I ask you for _____

_____

_____

I thank you for _____

_____

_____ Amen.

Heart Cookies

Ask an adult to help you make a batch of heart cookies for your family. When you serve them, break some of the cookies in half. Tell your family what you learned about a broken, sorry heart.

What You Need
2 cups (.48 L) butter, softened
1 cup (.24 L) powdered sugar
4 cups (.96 L) flour
2 cups (.48 L) quick-cooking oats
2 teaspoons (10 mL) vanilla extract
½ teaspoon (2.5 mL) almond extract
½ teaspoon (2.5 mL) salt
2 cups (.48 L) chocolate chips, melted

How to Do It
1. Preheat oven to 350°.
2. Cream butter and powdered sugar together in a mixing bowl.
3. Add flour, oats, vanilla, almond, and salt; mix well.
4. Roll out dough to ¼" (.6 cm) thickness.
5. Cut dough with a heart-shaped cookie cutter.
6. Place on ungreased baking sheets. Bake 12-15 minutes.
7. While cookies are warm, frost with the melted chocolate chips. Cool.

■ Theme for the Week: Confession

■ Key Verse for the Week

Forgive us our sins, for we also forgive every-one who sins against us.

—Luke 11:4

■ Bible Reading: Psalm 103:8-12

Far-giveness

Maybe you've heard someone say, "I'll forgive, but I won't forget!" Even after you've forgiven someone for gossiping about you, it's not always easy to forget the terrible words that were said.

God has a wonderful policy about forgiving and forgetting. Psalm 103:12 says, "As far as the east is from the west, so far has he removed our transgressions [sins] from us." God's forgiveness can be called far-giveness. He takes our sins and throws them as far as the east is from the west. That's too far to measure or even imagine.

God's promise in Psalm 103:10-12 is for you. Make it your personal prayer of confession by writing your name in the blanks.

He does not treat _____ as her sins deserve or repay _____ according to her iniquities. For as high as the heavens are above the earth, so great is his love for _____ who fears him; as far as the east is from the west, so far has he removed _____'s sins from her.

■ Something to Think About

When God forgives your sins, he throws them into the deepest sea and marks it with a "No Fishing" sign. Thank God for *far*-give-ness today.

Dear Jesus,

I praise you for _____

_____

_____

I'm sorry for _____

_____

_____

I ask you for _____

_____

_____

I thank you for _____

_____

_____ Amen.

Stargazing

Ask your family to join you tonight to study the stars. If the weather is nice, you can lie on a blanket or sit on the front porch. Here are some things to watch for:

- the first star
- the North Star (a bright star that appears almost directly above the North Pole)
- the Big Dipper (the two stars at the end of the bowl of the Big Dipper point to the North Star)
- star pictures

Tell your family that God *far*-gives your sins even farther than the highest star in the sky.

■ Theme for the Week: Confession

■ Key Verse for the Week

Forgive us our sins, for we also forgive everyone who sins against us.

—Luke 11:4

■ Bible Reading: Matthew 18:21-35

How Many Times?

Knock knock. Who's there? Banana. Banana who?

Knock knock. Who's there? Banana. Banana who?

Knock knock. Who's there? Orange. Orange who?

Orange you glad I didn't say banana again?

Does the way you forgive other people sound like a knock-knock joke? Have you ever said "I forgive you" without meaning what you said?

Pretend that your brother pulled all the sheets off your bed and emptied your dresser drawers in the middle of the bedroom. You'd probably be very mad at him! And what if it happened day after day? Your conversation might sound something like this:

First time: *"I messed up your room."* *"I know." "I'm sorry." "I forgive you."*

Second time: *"I messed up your room."* *"I know." "I'm sorry." "I forgive you."*

Third time: *"I messed up your room."* *"I know." "I'm sorry." "I forgive you."*

If this happened day after day it would be about as funny as the knock-knock joke!

The disciple Peter once asked Jesus how many times he had to forgive people. Peter thought he was being extra nice when he suggested seven times. What did Jesus answer? "Not seven times, but seventy-seven times" (Matthew 18:22). So if your brother was sincere each time he asked for your forgiveness, you'd have to keep forgiving him!

■ Something to Think About

Seventy-seven is not a magical number where you get to stop forgiving others when they hurt you! What it really means is that you may never, never stop forgiving.

Dear Jesus,

I praise you for _____

_____

_____

I'm sorry for _____

_____

_____

I ask you for _____

_____

_____

I thank you for _____

_____

_____ Amen.

Forgiveness Cards

Do you have someone you need to forgive? Maybe you have someone who you need to say "I'm sorry" to. Do it with a for-giveness card!

What You Need

9" x 12" piece of construction paper
Fabric scraps
Ribbon
Lace
Yarn
Buttons
Beads
Glitter
Sequins
Glue
Scissors
Markers or crayons

How to Do It

1. On the front of your card make a picture with your supplies. Be creative!
2. On the inside of the card use your markers or crayons and write a message of forgiveness or "I'm sorry."
3. Mail or bring your card to the person today!

■ Theme for the Week: Confession

■ Key Verse for the Week

Forgive us our sins, for we also forgive every-one who sins against us.

—Luke 11:4

■ Bible Reading: 1 John 1:5-10

Who Me? Couldn't Be!

Have you ever chanted this playground song?

> *Who stole the cookie from the cookie jar?*
> *_____ stole the cookie from the cookie jar.*
> *Who me?*
> *Yes you.*
> *Couldn't be!*
> *Then who?*

After that verse, the person who is accused of stealing the cookie blames someone else . . . and it goes on and on. No matter how many verses are sung, the message is the same: no one wants to admit that they stole the cookie from the cookie jar!

That's often the way it is in real life too. People don't like to admit it when they've done something wrong. But Jesus is the only one who has never done anything wrong. Everyone else is a sinner who needs forgiveness.

You can be sure God will forgive you when you tell God your sins. First John 1:9 says, "If we confess our sins, he is faithful and just and will forgive us our sins and purify us from all unrighteousness." God will forgive you because of Jesus! That's great news for all sinners, including cookie thieves!

■ Something to Think About

Everyone is a sinner. Here's the really important question to ask yourself: Am I a forgiven sinner?

_____Yes   __No

Dear Jesus,

I praise you for _____

_____

_____

I'm sorry for _____

_____

_____

I ask you for _____

_____

_____

I thank you for _____

_____

_____ Amen.

Forgiveness Reminder Activities

Depending on what climate you live in, do one of the following forgiveness reminder activities.

Snowy Climate

God makes sinners whiter than snow (Isaiah 1:18).

- Make snow angels. Lie backside down in the snow and swing your arms and legs back and forth.
- Build a snowman, snow girl, or snow house!
- Ask your parents or friends to join you in a fun snowball fight.

Warm Climate

When you do these activities, remember that God throws your sins into the deepest sea.

- Go fishing or swimming.
- Take a long bubble bath!

W E E K **3** T H R E E

■ Theme for the Week: Confession

■ Key Verse for the Week
Write the key verse for the week on the lines below.

_____

_____

_____

—Luke 11:4

■ This Week I Learned . . .

Sunday
Forgiveness has two parts. I ask God for forgiveness, and I am ready to forgive others (Luke 11:1-4).

Monday
Forgiveness is free because Jesus paid for my sins when he died on the cross and became alive again three days later (Isaiah 55:6-7).

Tuesday
When I tell God I'm sorry for my sins, I must do more than go through the motions. My confession has to come from the heart (Psalm 51:16-17).

Wednesday
God forgives and far-gives my sins by throwing them as far away as the east is from the west (Psalm 103:8-12).

Thursday
God never, ever wants me to stop forgiving others when they hurt me (Matthew 18:21-35).

Friday
Who me? Yes, me and everyone else too. Jesus is the only one who is not a sinner. The question I need to answer is, Am I a forgiven sinner? (1 John 1:5-10).

■ Something to Think About
What did you learn about forgiveness this week?

_____

_____

Dear Jesus,

I praise you for _____

_____

_____

I'm sorry for _____

_____

_____

I ask you for _____

_____

_____

I thank you for _____

_____

_____ Amen.

Shiny Clean Pennies

Because God forgives you, your sins are taken away and you are made clean. It's not magic—it's because of Jesus' death on the cross. Here's a trick to make dull pennies shiny clean. Show your friends and family your trick. When you're finished, tell them how God cleans the hearts of sinners.

What You Need

1 oz. lemon juice or vinegar
Small glass or paper cup
Dull penny

How to Do It

1. Pour lemon juice or vinegar into the paper cup.
2. Soak the penny for five minutes.
3. Take the shiny clean penny out of the glass.

■ Theme for the Week: Asking

■ Key Verse for the Week

Ask and it will be given to you; seek and you will find; knock and the door will be opened to you. For everyone who asks receives; he who seeks finds; and to him who knocks, the door will be opened.

—Matthew 7:7-8

■ Bible Reading: Matthew 7:7-8

Help!!!

Quick. What do you dial when there's an emergency like a fire or car accident? Right. The number is 911. You're only supposed to dial 911 when there's a real emergency.

Many people treat prayer like a 911 call. They only call on God in prayer when they need help. They usually don't talk to God unless there's an emergency and they need help immediately.

God wants you to stay in touch every day, not just when there's an emergency. God also wants you to ask for things. In fact, the Bible says that if you don't ask, you might not receive. "Ask and it will be given to you; seek and you will find; knock and the door will be opened to you. For everyone who asks receives; he who seeks finds; and to him who knocks, the door will be opened" (Matthew 7:7-8).

In response to your asking, God promises to answer. Sometimes the answer is yes and sometimes it's no. Do you know how God decides? By giving you whatever is best. It's true. Read it for yourself in Romans 8:28.

■ Something to Think About

When you call 911, you have to tell the operator who you are and where you're calling from. God not only knows who's calling but also what you're going to ask even before you begin asking!

Dear Jesus,

I praise you for _____

_____

_____

I'm sorry for _____

_____

_____

I ask you for _____

_____

_____

I thank you for _____

_____

_____ Amen.

Use markers, highlighters, glitter crayons, colored pencils,
and so on to color the theme word for the week.

ASKING

■ Theme for the Week: Asking

■ Key Verse for the Week

Ask and it will be given to you; seek and you will find; knock and the door will be opened to you. For everyone who asks receives; he who seeks finds; and to him who knocks, the door will be opened.

—*Matthew 7:7-8*

■ Bible Reading: Psalm 5:1-3

I Want It—Now!

When it comes to waiting for a special day like your birthday, Christmas, or a vacation, how patient are you? Check one:

___ a. Waiting is easy. I can wait for years for the special day to arrive.

___ b. Not a problem. I keep busy with other things while I'm waiting.

___ c. I want it to come, and I want it *now!*

When it comes to asking God for things in your prayers, how patient are you? Can you wait and wait for God's answer or do you want it right *now?*

The author of Psalm 5 talks about waiting for God's answer to prayers. In verse 3 he writes, "In the morning, O LORD, you hear my voice; in the morning I lay my requests before you and wait in expectation."

Waiting in expectation means that you expect God to answer your prayers. You know that God will give you an answer. Sometimes God answers immediately. Sometimes it takes years and years of prayer. You may not always get an answer right away, but God will answer.

■ Something to Think About

Here's a tip to help you wait in expectation. Write the date of your prayers in your journal. When God answers your prayers, you can go back in your journal and record the date and the answer.

Dear Jesus,

I praise you for _____
_____
_____

I'm sorry for _____
_____
_____

I ask you for _____
_____
_____

I thank you for _____
_____
_____ Amen.

Pizza Snack

Ask your family or friends if they'd like to taste a pizza snack. Expect them to answer yes! (If you know they don't like pizza, offer to fix another kind of snack.) Serve and enjoy.

What You Need
English muffins
Shredded cheddar or mozzarella cheese
Italian tomato or pizza sauce
Other pizza toppings (optional)

How to Do It
1. Ask an adult for permission to work in the kitchen.
2. Split the English muffins in half.
3. Spread a little sauce on each muffin half.
4. Sprinkle cheese over the sauce.
5. Add other pizza toppings (optional).
6. Broil pizzas until cheese melts (3-5 minutes) or microwave for 1-2 minutes.

■ Theme for the Week: Asking

■ Key Verse for the Week

Ask and it will be given to you; seek and you will find; knock and the door will be opened to you. For everyone who asks receives; he who seeks finds; and to him who knocks, the door will be opened.

—*Matthew 7:7-8*

■ Bible Reading: Luke 6:28-29

Sticks and Stones Are Not an Option

Do you have a hard time being nice to the bossy girls at school or the kid in your class who gossips about you? Maybe you can't even stand looking at the boy who teases you every noon hour. It's not always so easy to love everyone.

It's especially difficult to love your enemies. Enemies are people who attack or hurt others with their words and actions. Although God's daughters and sons should never harm people with their words and actions, they can't control what others say and do. Can you think of a neighbor or classmate who has hurt you this week or someone who attacks you with teasing?

Jesus has something very specific to say about what you should do to your enemies. It has nothing to do with sticks, stones, or name-calling. In Luke 6:28 Jesus says, "bless those who curse you, pray for those who mistreat you." Did you catch that? Jesus wants you to be nice to your enemies and pray for them! Through prayer, Jesus can turn enemies into friends!

■ Something to Think About

If you have an enemy who is hard to love, begin praying for her or him each day. After a week, you'll be amazed—it will be harder and harder to stay angry. Try it and see!

Dear Jesus,

I praise you for _____

_____

_____

I'm sorry for _____

_____

_____

I ask you for _____

_____

_____

I thank you for _____

_____

_____ Amen.

Missing Vowels Game

Y _ _ h _ v _ h _ _ rd th _ t _ t w _ s s _ _ d, "L _ v _ y _ _ r
n _ _ ghb _ r _ nd h _ t _ y _ _ r _ n _ my. B _ t _ t _ ll y _ _: L _ v _ y _ _ r
_ n _ m _ _ s _ nd pr _ y f _ r th _ s _ wh _ p _ rs _ c _ t _ y _ _, th _ t y _ _
m _ y b _ c _ ll _ d s _ ns _ f y _ _ r F _ th _ r _ n h _ _ v _ n."

—Matthew 5:43-45a

Can you figure out which vowels are missing without looking up the Bible verse? Here are the number of times each vowel is missing:

A - 14   E – 21   I – 6   O – 16   U – 10

■ Theme for the Week: Asking

■ Key Verse for the Week

Ask and it will be given to you; seek and you will find; knock and the door will be opened to you. For everyone who asks receives; he who seeks finds; and to him who knocks, the door will be opened.

—*Matthew 7:7-8*

■ Bible Reading: Matthew 6:9-13

I'm Starving!

Have you ever walked into the kitchen and announced, "I'm starving!"? Maybe even two hours after eating dinner? If so, your mom likely told you that it's not possible to be starving two hours after eating dinner. You may have been hungry, but chances are you weren't starving!

In Matthew 6:11 Jesus teaches us to pray "Give us today our daily bread." If you looked in your cupboards, you'd probably see more food than what you need for today. Maybe you'd even see enough food

for a week or more! Full cupboards make the words "I'm starving" hard to believe.

When Jesus prays about daily bread, he's talking about more than food. Jesus wants you to pray only for each day's needs. Some girls act like they're starving when they tell God all the things they want: "I need new roller blades; I need to go to the party Friday night; I need new jeans; I need a different book bag . . ."

Jesus wants you to pray for the bread you need today and the needs you have today. He may not give you everything you want, but he promises to give you everything you need!

■ Something to Think About

Are you really starving? The next time you say "I need . . . ," stop and ask yourself if you really need it or if it's something that you want.

Dear Jesus,

I praise you for _____
_____
_____

I'm sorry for _____
_____
_____

I ask you for _____
_____
_____

I thank you for _____
_____
_____ *Amen.*

Teddy Bear Biscuits

What You Need
One tube (7½ oz.) refrigerated buttermilk biscuits (you'll use nine out of ten biscuits to make three bears)
1 egg, beaten
2 tablespoons (30 mL) sugar
¼ teaspoon (1.2 mL) ground cinnamon
9 miniature semisweet chocolate chips
Cookie sheet

How to Do It
1. Ask an adult if you may work in the kitchen.
2. On a greased cookie sheet, shape one biscuit into an oval for the body.
3. Cut one biscuit into four pieces and shape into balls for arms and legs.
4. Cut one biscuit into one large and two small pieces for the head and ears.
5. Brush bears with egg and sprinkle with the mixed cinnamon and sugar.
6. Bake at 425° for 8-10 minutes.
7. While bears are still warm, place chocolate chips for eyes and mouth.

—Reprinted with permission from *Quick Cooking* magazine, P.O. Box 992, Greendale WI 53129.

■ **Theme for the Week: Asking**

■ **Key Verse for the Week**

Ask and it will be given to you; seek and you will find; knock and the door will be opened to you. For everyone who asks receives; he who seeks finds; and to him who knocks, the door will be opened.

—*Matthew 7:7-8*

■ **Bible Reading: Ephesians 6:18-20**

Making My List, Praying It Twice

Who's on your list of people to pray for? Hopefully your list includes family and friends, your enemies, and saints. That's right . . . saints.

Ephesians 6:18b says "always keep praying for all the saints." Just who are these saints? you're probably wondering. Do they walk around wearing white robes and golden halos?

Saints are people who love, worship, and serve Jesus. Saints can be old or young, sick or healthy, rich or poor. The one require-ment of a saint is that he or she believes in the Lord. If you love Jesus, you're a saint too!

Today's Bible passage tells us that God wants Christians to pray for all of the saints. Here's a short list to get you started with some of the saints that you can be praying for each day:

- People in nursing homes
- Missionaries and pastors
- Your church school class
- Christian friends at school
- Church janitors
- Persecuted Christians

■ **Something to Think About**

When you've made your prayer list, check it twice. Make sure it includes the saints!

Dear Jesus,

I praise you for _____

_____

_____

I'm sorry for _____

_____

_____

I ask you for _____

_____

_____

I thank you for _____

_____

_____ *Amen.*

Prayer Poster

Have you been praying for someone who is sick? Show this person you care by making a prayer poster. If possible, deliver your prayer poster in person.

What You Need

Posterboard, Markers, Glue, Paper

How to Do It

1. Cut five or more large hearts out of paper.
2. Write "I'm praying for you!" across the top of the poster.
3. Write the messages like these on the hearts (or make up your own).
   - To [fill in sick person's name] From [fill in your name].
   - I'm praying that you'll feel well soon.
   - Psalm 27:1 (write out the whole verse).
   - Jesus loves you and so do I!
   - Matthew 28:20 (write out the whole verse).
4. Glue the hearts on the posterboard.

■ Theme for the Week: Asking

■ Key Verse for the Week

Ask and it will be given to you; seek and you will find; knock and the door will be opened to you. For everyone who asks receives; he who seeks finds; and to him who knocks, the door will be opened.

—*Matthew 7:7-8*

■ Bible Reading: Luke 18:1-7

Praying Over and Over and Over Again!

You: *Mom, can I have a candy bar?*

Mom: *Not now. You'll spoil your appetite and it's almost time to eat.*

You: *Please, I promise that I'll still eat my whole dinner.*

Mom: *No, you don't need to fill up on sugar before our meal.*

You: *They're not very big. How about I only eat half?*

Mom: *I said no.*

You: *You don't understand. I'm so hungry. I'm starving!*

Mom: *Fine. Have one, but you will eat every bite of your dinner too!*

Have you ever had a conversation like this with your mom or dad? Did you know Jesus wants you to pray like that? Luke 18:1 says, "Then Jesus told his disciples a parable to show them that they should always pray and not give up."

Jesus told them a story about a persistent widow. She kept asking the judge to help her. Finally, even though the judge didn't feel like it, he helped her.

When it seems like God isn't answering your prayers, don't give up. Keep on praying like the persistent widow. Ask God over and over and over again. It's OK to do that—the Bible tells you so!

■ Something to Think About

Make it your goal to be a persistent pray-er!

Dear Jesus,

I praise you for _____

_____

_____

I'm sorry for _____

_____

_____

I ask you for _____

_____

_____

I thank you for _____

_____

_____ Amen.

A-MAZE-Ing

Are you persistent enough to get through this maze? Keep trying over and over and over again until you figure it out!

■ Theme for the Week: Asking

■ Key Verse for the Week
Write the key verse for the week on the lines below.

_____

_____

_____

_____

—Matthew 7:7-8

■ This Week I Learned . . .

Sunday
Prayer is not supposed to be a 911 call. I should be praying every day, not just when I'm in trouble (Matthew 7:7-8).

Monday
When I pray, I should expect God to answer. I may have to wait, but God will give me what's best (Psalm 5:1-3).

Tuesday
Although it's not easy, God wants me to pray for my enemies and show them God's love (Luke 6:28-29).

Wednesday
There's a difference between needs and wants. God promises to give me everything I need for each day (Matthew 6:9-13).

Thursday
My prayer list should always include the saints. Saints are the people who love and worship Jesus (Ephesians 6:18-20).

Friday
I need to be a persistent pray-er. Jesus tells me to ask over and over and over again (Luke 18:1-7).

■ Something to Think About
List some of the people and items you prayed about this week (enemies, other Christians, and some of your needs).

_____

_____

_____

Dear Jesus,

I praise you for _____

_____

_____

I'm sorry for _____

_____

_____

I ask you for _____

_____

_____

I thank you for _____

_____

_____ Amen.

D . . . D . . . D . . . Discover the Message

Solve the puzzle. Use the hints if you must!

ADSDKDADNDDDIDTDWDIDLDLDBDEDGDIDVDEDNDTDODYDODUD;SDEDEDKDADNDDD
YDODUDWDIDLDLDLFDIDNDDD;KDNDODCDKDADNDDDTDHDEDDDODODRDWDIDLDLDB
DEDODPDEDNDEDDDTDODYDODUD.FDODRDEDVDEDRDYDODNDEDWDHDODADSDKD
SDRDEDCDEDIDVDEDSD;HDEDWDHDODSDEDEDKDSDFDIDNDDDSD;ADNDDDTDODHDID
MDWDHDODKDNDODCDKDSD,TDHDEDDDODODRDWDIDLDLDLDBDE DODPDEDNDEDDD.

First hint: Don't give up! If you need help, *ask* (we learned about asking this week, right?) a parent or friend to help you.

Second hint: There are way too many Ds in the puzzle. Still stumped? Look at the key verse for the week.

■ Theme for the Week: Thankfulness

■ Key Verse for the Week

Let them give thanks to the LORD for his unfailing love and his wonderful deeds. . . .
—Psalm 107:8

■ Bible Reading: Psalm 100

Thanks, God!

Have you ever walked into church with a grumpy attitude? Maybe you couldn't find your favorite necklace or maybe you got in trouble for getting mud on the car seat.

The person who wrote Psalm 100:4 expresses a different kind of attitude: "Enter his gates with thanksgiving and his courts with praise; give thanks to him and praise his name." If the psalmist were writing this psalm today, it might sound like this: "I will open the church doors with thanksgiving and walk through the church praising God's name."

Why should you begin the week thanking and praising God in church? You'll find the answer in verse 5: "For the LORD is good and his love endures forever; his faithfulness continues through all generations."

You can show you're thankful for God's love by your attitude in church. So next Sunday, "worship the LORD with gladness." Smile! Sing joyful songs. Think about the words, and sing out loud! Open the church doors with a thankful heart. Walk through the church and praise the Lord!

■ Something to Think About

When you went to church today were you

____ grumpy   ____ thankful   ____ bored

Guess What, Jesus?

Dear Jesus,

I praise you for _____

_____

_____

I'm sorry for _____

_____

_____

I ask you for _____

_____

_____

I thank you for _____

_____

_____ Amen.

Sunday Place Mats

What You Need

Typing paper or construction paper, Markers, Contact paper

Enter His Gates with Thanksgiving and His courts with Praise Give Thanks to Him and bless His name Psalm 100:16

How to Do It

1. On a piece of paper write down Psalm 100:4: *Enter his gates with thanksgiving and his courts with praise; give thanks to him and praise his name.* Use your markers to create a colorful background.
2. Place the sheet of paper between two layers of clear contact paper so that spills can be easily washed off.
3. Use your place mat on Sundays to help remind you to have a thankful heart when you go to church.
4. Maybe you could surprise your family by making a place mat for each family member!

■ Theme for the Week: Thankfulness

■ Key Verse for the Week

Let them give thanks to the LORD for his unfailing love and his wonderful deeds. . . .
—*Psalm 107:8*

■ Bible Reading: Psalm 107:1, 8, 21-22, 31

Thank-FULL-ness

Have you ever been so full of thanks that the "thank yous" kept spilling from your mouth over and over? Maybe your mom or dad surprised you with a puppy or an extra-special vacation.

Thank-FULL-ness is just what it sounds like—it means being full of thanks! Today's Bible reading tells you who should receive your thanks. "Give thanks to the LORD, for he is good; his love endures forever" (Psalm 107:1).

Read verses 8, 21, and 31 again. Did you notice how the writer of Psalm 107 repeats himself? The psalmist is thankful for God's unfailing love and for the wonderful things God does.

The Bible is still true today. Like the psalmist, you can be thank-FULL because God loves you! You can also be thank-FULL for the wonderful things God does for you. So whenever you feel thank-less, try reading Psalm 107:8. Let it remind you how much God loves you. And then think about some of the things God has done for you. When you do those two things God will fill you to the top with thank-FULL-ness!

■ Something to Think About

When you're thank-FULL, your thanks should start from your toes, go up to your nose, and spill out with a great big smile!

Dear Jesus,

I praise you for _____
_____
_____

I'm sorry for _____
_____
_____

I ask you for _____
_____
_____

I thank you for _____
_____
_____ Amen.

Funny Faced Feet

What You Need
Washable markers
A brave parent, brother, sister, or friend (Or do this activity with a group of friends. The more people the more giggles!)

How to Do It
Draw pictures on the bottom of each other's feet. Be prepared for lots of tickling and laughing!

Funny Faced Treat

What You Need
Round party rye bread (look in the deli section of your grocery store)
Cheese spread
Raisins

How to Do It
Spread cheese on the bread. Use the raisins to make the eyes and mouth. (Make sure the mouth has a great big smile!)

■ Theme for the Week: Thankfulness

■ Key Verse for the Week

Let them give thanks to the LORD for his unfailing love and his wonderful deeds. . . .
—*Psalm 107:8*

■ Bible Reading: Luke 17:11-19

What Do You Say?

Remember opening Christmas presents when you were little? After each gift, you'd hear, "What do you say?" And you would answer, "Thank you!" When you receive gifts today, do you still have to be reminded to say thanks? Hopefully not!

Today's Bible reading tells the story of ten men who had leprosy, a terrible skin disease. In those days, people who had leprosy had to stay far away from their family and friends. These ten men called out to Jesus from a distance and asked him to heal them. What do you think Jesus did? Luke 17:14 says, "When he saw them, he said, 'Go, show yourselves to the priests.' And as they went, they were cleansed."

These ten lepers must have been so thankful for this incredible miracle, right? But check out verse 15. How many of them came back to thank and praise Jesus for what he had done? One. Only one out of ten came back to Jesus and said thank you.

Have you ever forgotten to say thanks like the nine lepers? Think about some of the good things God has done for you. And then give thanks and praise to God. What do you say?

■ Something to Think About

In your prayers today be very specific about what you're thankful for. For instance, instead of saying, "Thanks for everything in the world," thank Jesus for a few special things you're thinking of: your mom and dad (even your brother, who's always teasing you), a fresh blanket of fluffy snow, a sleepover at your best friend's. . . . Praise Jesus for each of these good gifts!

Dear Jesus,

I praise you for _____

_____

_____

I'm sorry for _____

_____

_____

I ask you for _____

_____

_____

I thank you for _____

_____

_____ Amen.

A to Z—Thankfully!

List the things you're thankful for from A to Z. The first couple of
letters have examples to get you started.

A *rt set* _____

B *ible* _____

C _____

D _____

E _____

F _____

G _____

H _____

I _____

J _____

K _____

L _____

M _____

N _____

O _____

P _____

Q _____

R _____

S _____

T _____

U _____

V _____

W _____

X _____

Y _____

Z _____

■ Theme for the Week: Thankfulness

■ Key Verse for the Week

Let them give thanks to the LORD for his unfailing love and his wonderful deeds. . . .
—Psalm 107:8

■ Bible Reading: 1 Thessalonians 5:16-18

Broccoli? I Don't Think So!

I can think of a few things that I'm not thankful for: chicken pox . . . broccoli . . . spiders . . . storms . . . braces . . .

When you're sick in bed covered from head to toe with itchy chicken pox or when a creepy crawler scurries up your bedroom wall, do you have to be thankful?

Look at verse 18 of 1 Thessalonians 5. The apostle Paul writes: "Give thanks in all circumstances, for this is God's will for you in Christ Jesus." And in Ephesians 5:20 he writes: "always giving thanks to God the Father for everything, in the name of our Lord Jesus Christ."

Wow! God wants you to be thankful in *all* circumstances. No matter what you look like, where you live, what school you go to, who your parents are . . . God says to be thankful.

Paul practiced what he preached about thankfulness. Many of his letters that we read in our Bibles were written by Paul when he was behind bars. If Paul could be thankful while he was in jail, can you find reasons to be thankful for spiders, storms, and, yes, even broccoli?

■ Something to Think About

Some days it's easier to be thankful than other days. No matter what kind of a day this is for you, ask God to give you a thankful heart. If things are going great, give joyful thanks! If you're having a bad day, make a point of giving thanks in spite of it. Remember that Jesus is with you in good times and bad.

Dear Jesus,

I praise you for _____

_____

_____

I'm sorry for _____

_____

_____

I ask you for _____

_____

_____

I thank you for _____

_____

_____ Amen.

Spider Snack

What You Need
2 wafer cookies
 (spider body)
2 teaspoons frosting
8 small sections of
 licorice whip
 (spider legs)
2 chocolate chips
 (spider eyes)

How to Do It
1. Spread the frosting on two cookies and make a cookie sandwich.
2. Insert the eight "legs" around the spider's body.
3. For the eyes, dab a little frosting on top of the body and set the chocolate chips on top.
4. Serve this tasty treat to your family and friends. Tell them what you're learning this week about being thankful for everything—even when you have to deal with spiders!

■ Theme for the Week: Thankfulness

■ Key Verse for the Week

Let them give thanks to the LORD for his unfailing love and his wonderful deeds. . . .
—Psalm 107:8

■ Bible Reading: Colossians 3:15-18

Thanksliving

Have you ever heard someone use the word "thanksliving"? It's right there in Colossians 3:17: "And whatever you do, whether in word or deed, do it all in the name of the Lord Jesus, giving thanks to God the Father through him."

Giving thanks *(thanks)* in whatever you do in word or deed *(living)* is *thanksliving*.

Compare these two situations and pick the one that shows thanksliving:

1. As you walk into the kitchen for breakfast your dad says, "Good morning!" You flop into the chair and whine, "Cold cereal again?"

2. As you walk into the kitchen for breakfast your dad says, "Good morning!" You sit in your chair and answer, "Hi, Dad. How are you today?"

It's not hard to see which of those two scenarios you'd pick to show a life of thanksliving. Thanksliving doesn't mean you have to walk around the house all day saying thank you (although that's not a bad idea!). But it does mean that whatever you do or say, your attitude shows Jesus your thankful heart.

■ Something to Think About

Write a note to Jesus about one way that you're going to try to live a life of thanksliving today. Put the note in your Bible by Colossians 3.

Dear Jesus,

I praise you for _____

_____

_____

I'm sorry for _____

_____

_____

I ask you for _____

_____

_____

I thank you for _____

_____

_____ Amen.

Thanksliving Word Search

This word search includes things you do each day. Find the words and live a life of thanksliving today!

CLEAN	LISTEN	SLEEP
DRAW	PLAY	SMILE
DRESS	PRAY	STUDY
EAT	READ	TALK
HELP	RUN	WALK
JOKE	SING	WATCH
JUMP	SKIP	WRITE
LEARN		

S	E	S	T	U	D	Y	C	Y	N	T
N	S	K	W	A	L	K	A	R	A	E
W	E	E	O	K	Q	R	A	E	L	T
R	C	T	R	J	P	E	C	I	L	A
I	I	H	S	D	L	L	M	K	S	L
T	N	O	G	I	E	S	R	Y	R	K
E	W	N	P	A	L	P	Y	E	A	A
Y	I	M	N	P	S	D	E	A	A	D
S	U	H	L	T	Z	K	R	E	L	D
J	S	E	N	N	U	R	I	A	L	P
K	H	W	A	T	C	H	H	P	W	S

■ Theme for the Week: Thankfulness

■ Key Verse for the Week

Let them give thanks to the Lord for his unfailing love and his wonderful deeds. . . .
—*Psalm 107:8*

■ Bible Reading: Ephesians 1:15-16

Never, Ever Stop!

After you've eaten the 3,890th dinner that your mom or dad cooked for you—whether it's hot dogs, fried chicken, or grilled cheese sandwiches—do you still have to say thanks? If you've already thanked her 3,889 times, he probably already knows you're thankful. So do you still need to say thank you? You probably guessed the answer already—it's yes!

But what's even more important than saying thanks to your mom or dad each day for food is saying thanks each day for God's blessings. God never tires of hearing your thanks.

In Ephesians 1:16 Paul says, "I have not stopped giving thanks for you, remembering you in my prayers." Each day he thanked God for the people who lived in Ephesus. Paul could have said thanks to God once or twice, but the people's faith in Jesus made Paul so thankful that he never stopped thanking God.

Parents, teachers, police officers, pastors, doctors, farmers, friends, missionaries, homes, clothing, toys, food, Bibles . . . the list of people and things to be thankful for is endless. You can show your thankful heart for all these and more by repeating your thanks to God for the blessings that mean the most to you. Never, ever stop giving thanks!

■ Something to Think About

Why not thank God for the same things you did yesterday? It's a good way to let God know how much these gifts mean to you!

Dear Jesus,

I praise you for _____

_____

_____

I'm sorry for _____

_____

_____

I ask you for _____

_____

_____

I thank you for _____

_____

_____ Amen.

Thank-You Gifts

God never gets tired of hearing you say thank you again and again. Can you think of someone else who would love to hear your thanks? Here are some ideas: the person who cleans your school, librarian, pastor, church school teacher.

Choose a person and pick one of the following ways to say thank you:

- Make a card.
- Telephone or e-mail the person.
- Make and deliver chocolate chip cookies.
- Draw and send a picture.
- Give him or her a hug!

■ Theme for the Week: Thankfulness

■ Key Verse for the Week

Write the key verse for the week on the lines below:

_____

_____

_____

—*Psalm 107:8*

■ This Week I Learned . . .

Sunday
It's important to begin my week thanking and praising God in church (Psalm 100).

Monday
Thank-FULL-ness means being full of thanks for God's love and all the wonderful things God does for me (Psalm 107:1, 8, 21-22, 31).

Tuesday
I need to be like the one leper who went back and praised Jesus after being healed. I need to thank God for specific blessings without being reminded (Luke 17:11-19).

Wednesday
God wants me to be thankful in all circumstances—even when things happen that I don't like! (1 Thessalonians 5:16-18).

Thursday
Whatever I do and say needs to be done with thanksgiving, or should I say thanksliving? (Colossians 3:15-18).

Friday
God wants me to say thanks over and over for the blessings that mean the most to me (Ephesians 1:15-16).

■ Something to Think About

List some of the people and things you're most thankful to God for:

_____

_____

_____

_____

Dear Jesus,

I praise you for _____

_____

_____

I'm sorry for _____

_____

_____

I ask you for _____

_____

_____

I thank you for _____

_____

_____ Amen.

Magnetic Hearts

Let your heart magnet remind you to show Jesus a heart that is full of thankfulness. Use it to display your favorite art projects.

What You Need
Small wooden heart from a craft store
Paints and paint brushes
Magnet strip
Sequins, lace, or other decorations (optional)

How to Do It
1. Paint the heart.
2. After it's dry, paint your name across the heart.
3. Glue sequins, lace, or other decorations around your name if you like.
4. Attach the magnet to the back of the heart.

■ **Theme for the Week: Compassion**

■ **Key Verse for the Week**

Therefore, as God's chosen people, holy and dearly loved, clothe yourselves with compassion, kindness, humility, gentleness and patience.

—Colossians 3:12

■ **Bible Reading: Colossians 3:12-14**

Compassion Clothes

Are you wearing your compassion clothes?

My what??? Just what kind of clothes are these, anyway? you're probably thinking. You won't find compassion clothes in the mall, and even the most talented grandmas can't sew them. But whenever you wear compassion clothes you'll look beautiful—because you'll glow with the love of Jesus.

If you'd like some compassion clothes for yourself, check out Colossians 3:12, the key verse for the week. The first part of the verse says, "Therefore, as God's chosen people [that's you], holy and dearly loved, clothe yourselves with compassion."

God wants you to *wear* compassion. You can't pull compassion clothes over your head like a sweatshirt or pull them onto your feet like socks. But people will know you're wearing your compassion clothes when they see you helping others and hear your caring words. Whenever you reach out to others with the love of Jesus, you're wearing compassion clothes!

■ **Something to Think About**

Set out the clothes you're going to wear tomorrow morning. Write the word "compassion" on a notecard and place the card on top of the clothing as a reminder to put on your compassion clothes too. That's far more important than what color shirt you're going to wear!

Dear Jesus,

I praise you for _____

_____

_____

I'm sorry for _____

_____

_____

I ask you for _____

_____

_____

I thank you for _____

_____

_____ Amen.

Painted T-Shirts

What You Need

White cotton T-shirt
Large piece of cardboard
Fabric pen and fine brush
Fabric paints (a few of your
　favorite colors)
Pearlized fabric paint (another
　color)

How to Do It

1. Wash the T-shirt and have an adult iron it.
2. Put cardboard inside the T-shirt so the fabric paint won't run through.
3. With the fabric pen, draw different sizes of hearts on front of the shirt.
4. Use the fine brush to paint in the hearts with the fabric paints.
5. When paint is dry, outline each heart with small dots using the pearlized fabric paint.

■ Theme for the Week: Compassion

■ Key Verse for the Week

Therefore, as God's chosen people, holy and dearly loved, clothe yourselves with compassion, kindness, humility, gentleness and patience.

—*Colossians 3:12*

■ Bible Reading: Psalm 145:8-11

Two Feet, Hairy Feet, No Feet

Did you know that God has compassion on you? When you're lonely, God is compassionate. When you've sinned, God is slow to anger. When you're hurting, God is rich in love. God cares for and shows compassion to *all* people. It doesn't matter if they're tall or short, dark-haired or blonde, graceful or clumsy. God doesn't care if people live in big or small houses or if they're popular or not-so-popular at school.

God also has compassion for creation. God cares for mighty oceans and tiny flowers; for gigantic elephants and for bugs that have two feet, hairy feet, or no feet!

No one deserves God's compassion and rich love, yet God gives it generously to people day after day. Psalm 145:8-9 says, "The LORD is gracious and compassionate, slow to anger and rich in love. The LORD is good to all; he has compassion on all he has made." In your prayers today, praise God's loving care for you and all God's creatures.

■ Something to Think About

How can you show God how thankful you are for his compassion? One way is by caring for others and for the world God made. Think of one specific way you can help care for the world today. Write your idea on the line below, and then do it! *Hint:* If you need ideas, take a walk outside. See any trash that needs to be picked up? Do you have a neighbor that could use a hand with weeding the garden or raking leaves? Does your dog need some exercise?

_____

Dear Jesus,

I praise you for _____

_____

_____

I'm sorry for _____

_____

_____

I ask you for _____

_____

_____

I thank you for _____

_____

_____ Amen.

Banana Bug

Help your friends and family make banana bugs and tell them about God's compassion for people and the creation—even bugs!

What You Need
A not-so-ripe banana
12 pretzel sticks
Peanut butter
Raisins

How to Do It
1. Peel the banana and place it on a plate.
2. Poke six pretzel sticks on each side of the banana for the bug's legs.
3. Put two pretzel sticks on one end of the banana for the bug's antennae.
4. Put dabs of peanut butter along the bug's back to "glue" the raisins in place.
5. Use peanut butter for the bug's eyes.

■ Theme for the Week: Compassion

■ Key Verse for the Week

Therefore, as God's chosen people, holy and dearly loved, clothe yourselves with compassion, kindness, humility, gentleness and patience.

—Colossians 3:12

■ Bible Reading: 1 Peter 3:8-10

Are You Playing the Right Note?

Do you play the piano or some other musical instrument? If so, chances are your mom or dad or teacher sometimes says, "You hit the wrong note!" while you're practicing. Teachers or parents don't even have to see the music or be in the same room to know when you play a wrong note. They can tell it's not right because of how it sounds. The notes aren't in harmony with each other.

Harmony is created when all the notes in a song sound good together. But even if you're not much of a musician, you need to live in harmony—with other people. Living in harmony with others means working and playing together in peace.

First Peter 3:8 gives four steps to living in harmony with one another:

- Be sympathetic. When someone is happy, be happy with them. When someone is sad, be sad with them.
- Love as sisters and brothers. Love each other like Jesus loves you.
- Be compassionate. Let your words and actions show others how much you care for them.
- Be humble. Being humble is the opposite of being proud. It's impossible to live in harmony if you think you're better than everyone!

So keep on practicing. Your music—and your life—will be in tune!

■ Something to Think About

When God sees you living in harmony with those around you, you'll always be playing the right note. It's music to God's ears!

Dear Jesus,

I praise you for _____

_____

_____

I'm sorry for _____

_____

_____

I ask you for _____

_____

_____

I thank you for _____

_____

_____ Amen.

Making Harmony

What You Need
Jars or drinking glasses (eight of them)
Spoon
Water

How to Do It

1. On a table, line up the jars or glasses in a row.
2. Beginning on the left, fill the first glass almost to the top with water.
3. Fill the second glass a little bit less than the first one. Do this until all the glasses have water in them. Your last glass should only have a small amount on the bottom.
4. Tap a spoon against the jars. It should sound like a musical scale.
5. Experiment by sounding out "Row, Row, Row Your Boat."
6. Play your song for another person and tell them what you learned today about living in harmony with others.

■ Theme for the Week: Compassion

■ Key Verse for the Week

Therefore, as God's chosen people, holy and dearly loved, clothe yourselves with compassion, kindness, humility, gentleness and patience.

—Colossians 3:12

■ Bible Reading: Psalm 103:1-5

In Sickness or in Health

Can you remember the last time you were sick? Your parents probably gave you chicken noodle soup, ginger ale, medicine, and a warm blanket. You probably got extra hugs too. Parents tend to be even more compassionate than usual when you are sick.

Although moms and dads are compassionate, no one is more compassionate than God, your heavenly Father. Psalm 103:4 says God "crowns you with love and compassion."

God loves you so much! It's difficult to grasp and understand the depth of God's love and compassion for you. God erases the bad things you've done (Psalm 103:3). God won't leave you when you're sick (Psalm 103:3). God is there when you're healthy and happy; he "satisfies your desires with good things" (Psalm 103:5).

Think about God's compassion. Can you almost feel Jesus' loving arms wrapping around you? God promises to always care for you—in sickness and in health—yesterday, today, tomorrow, and forever.

■ Something to Think About

The next time someone is taking care of you while you're sick, remember that your compassionate heavenly Father is with you too!

Dear Jesus,

I praise you for _____

_____

_____

I'm sorry for _____

_____

_____

I ask you for _____

_____

_____

I thank you for _____

_____

_____ Amen.

Get-Well Projects

Do you or your mom or dad know someone who is sick at home or in the hospital? Choose one of these ways to show your compassion and to brighten his or her day:

- Pick some flowers or spend your allowance money to buy flowers and deliver them in person.
- For a sick child, buy a special stuffed animal. Bring your favorite book along and read to her or bring a board game and play with her.
- If the sick person is a mom with young children, offer to babysit for an afternoon or for a couple of hours in the evening. If she's resting at home, try to do quiet activities.
- Make a card that says you're praying for him or her. Write out Psalm 103:2-4 on the card.

■ Theme for the Week: Compassion

■ Key Verse for the Week

Therefore, as God's chosen people, holy and dearly loved, clothe yourselves with compassion, kindness, humility, gentleness and patience.

—*Colossians 3:12*

■ Bible Reading: Matthew 15:32-38

But . . . But . . . But . . .

For three days, Jesus sat on a mountainside with four thousand people. They brought to him the lame, the blind, the mute, and many others in need of healing. Jesus showed compassion for them by making the lame people walk, the blind see, and the mute talk.

After three days, the food that the people had brought with them was almost gone. They were very hungry! Jesus gathered his disciples around and said, "I have compassion for these people; they have already been with me three days and have nothing to eat. I do not want to send them away hungry, or they may collapse on the way" (Matthew 15:32).

And what did the disciples say? But . . . but . . . but . . . where could we get enough bread in this remote place to feed such a crowd? (verse 33). There were no grocery stores nearby, no cupboards full of food. They had nothing except seven loaves of bread and a few fish. The disciples gave what they had, and Jesus took care of the rest. That bread and fish fed four thousand people, and when they finished eating there were seven baskets of leftovers!

■ Something to Think About

There are so many people who need your compassion. "But . . . but . . . but . . . " you might be thinking, "I can't help them." Remember what the disciples learned—if you give him what you have, Jesus will take care of the rest.

Dear Jesus,

I praise you for _____

_____

_____

I'm sorry for _____

_____

_____

I ask you for _____

_____

_____

I thank you for _____

_____

_____ *Amen.*

Compassion Ideas

Pick one of the following ways to show compassion to someone this week. Circle the number of the one you choose.

1. Bake chocolate chip cookies and bring them to a busy mom or an elderly neighbor who doesn't have grandchildren living nearby.
2. Ask your mom or dad if you could earn some extra money. Take the money and give it to an organization that helps needy children.
3. Go to a nursing home or to an elderly neighbor and chat for a while. Seniors really enjoy talking with young people. Don't know what to talk about? Ask questions about what the person liked to do when he or she was your age . . . and share some of your own interests.
4. Surprise your dad, mom, brother, or sister by doing a job that you normally are not responsible for (like making your sister's bed or taking out the garbage without being asked . . . you get the idea!).

■ Theme for the Week: Compassion

■ Key Verse for the Week

Therefore, as God's chosen people, holy and dearly loved, clothe yourselves with compassion, kindness, humility, gentleness and patience.

—*Colossians 3:12*

■ Bible Reading: Luke 15:11-24

The Perfect Gift

Jesus told the story of a man with two sons. The youngest son asked his father for his share of the estate and the father gave it to him. Not long after, the son took his father's money, went to a distant country, and squandered every last coin.

Soon the son became very hungry. To earn money to eat, he worked for a pig farmer. When he saw that the pigs were getting more food than he did, he came to his senses. He decided to go back to his dad and say he was sorry.

"So he got up and went to his father. But while he was still a long way off, his father saw him and was filled with compassion for him; he ran to his son, threw his arms around him and kissed him" (Luke 15:20).

Wow! That son deserved to be punished, but the father gave him the gift of compassion. That's just like our Father in heaven! You and I deserve to be punished for our sins, but our heavenly Father gives us the perfect gift of compassion, Jesus Christ.

■ Something to Think About

Jesus died on the cross to take the punishment for your sins. Three days later he became alive again! Thank God today for Jesus Christ, the perfect gift of compassion.

Dear Jesus,

I praise you for _____

_____

_____

I'm sorry for _____

_____

_____

I ask you for _____

_____

_____

I thank you for _____

_____

_____ Amen.

Compassion Cake

What You Need
Cake mix
Frosting
Baking pan (9" x 13")

How to Do It
1. Ask an adult for permission to bake a cake.
2. Mix the cake batter according to the instructions.
3. Bake the cake in a 9" x 13" pan.
4. After it's cool, carefully remove the cake from the pan.
5. Cut the cross out of the cake according to the diagram. Frost.
6. Cut the "extra" cake that is not part of the cross into serving-size squares. Frost the squares to look like gifts.
7. Share the cake with your friends and family and tell them what you learned about God's perfect gift.

■ Theme for the Week: Compassion

■ Key Verse for the Week

Write the key verse for the week on the lines below.

_____

_____

_____

_____

—Colossians 3:12

■ This Week I Learned . . .

Sunday
Compassion clothes can't be bought or sewn, but Christians need to wear them every day (Colossians 3:12-14).

Monday
God shows love and compassion to everyone and everything he has made. It doesn't matter if they have two feet, hairy feet, or no feet! (Psalm 145:8-11).

Tuesday
To live in harmony with others, I must be sympathetic, loving, compassionate, and humble (1 Peter 3:8-10).

Wednesday
God's compassion for me will never stop in sickness or in health—today, tomorrow, and forever (Psalm 103:1-5).

Thursday
There are no ifs, ands, or buts about it, Jesus wants me to always show compassion to others (Matthew 15:32-38).

Friday
Instead of punishing me for my sins, God gives me a perfect gift of compassion, Jesus Christ (Luke 15:11-24).

■ Something to Think About

List some of the ways to show compassion to others you've learned about this week:

_____

_____

_____

Dear Jesus,

I praise you for _____

_____

_____

I'm sorry for _____

_____

_____

I ask you for _____

_____

_____

I thank you for _____

_____

_____ Amen.

Color this week's theme word. Use markers, crayons, colored pencils, or paint. Have fun!

■ **Theme for the Week: Faith**

■ **Key Verse for the Week**

Believe in the Lord Jesus, and you will be saved—you and your household.
—*Acts 16:31*

■ **Bible Reading: Acts 16:25-31**

It's All in Your Head (and Heart!)

Paul and Silas were in jail, singing and praying to God. Suddenly there was a terrible earthquake. The prison doors flew open and the jailer woke up. He was so afraid that the prisoners had escaped that he grabbed his sword and was about to kill himself.

When Paul saw what the jailer was going to do, he shouted, "Don't harm yourself! We are all here!" (Acts 16:28). The jailer was so surprised that the prisoners didn't try to escape! He realized that Paul and Silas had faith in a God that he didn't know. The jailer ran to them, fell before them, and said, "Sirs, what must I do to be saved?" (Acts 16:30).

Paul and Silas answered, "Believe in the Lord Jesus, and you will be saved—you and your household" (Acts 16:31). Believing in Jesus is called faith.

True faith is in your head and heart. In order to have faith like Paul, Silas, and the jailer, you must

- Know Jesus as your Savior (your head).
- Trust that Jesus saved you from your sins (your heart).

Thank God today for the gift of faith!

■ **Something to Think About**

True faith in a Christian's life must come from the head (knowing Jesus) and the heart (trusting in Jesus). You can't have one without the other.

Dear Jesus,

I praise you for _____

_____

_____

I'm sorry for _____

_____

_____

I ask you for _____

_____

_____

I thank you for _____

_____

_____ Amen.

Head and Heart Maze

Faith requires knowing Jesus (with your head) and trusting in him (with your heart). This maze has two beginnings and one end. Find your way from the head to faith and from the heart to faith.

■ Theme for the Week: Faith

■ Key Verse for the Week

Believe in the Lord Jesus, and you will be saved—you and your household.

—Acts 16:31

■ Bible Reading: Hebrews 11:1, 6

Not Seeing Is Believing!

Have you ever flown a kite or had a homework assignment blow away in the wind?

_____ Yes   _____ No

If you marked yes, you believe that wind is real.

Are you a person who has to see things with your eyes in order to believe it's really real?

_____ Yes   _____ No

If you said yes, then you must not really believe wind is real because you can't see the wind! You can see leaves, dust, and lost homework assignments blowing in the wind, but you can't see the wind.

Some people don't believe in Jesus because they've never seen him. They think that if they can't see him with their eyes, then he must not be real. Hebrews 11:1 says, "Now faith is being sure of what we hope for and certain of what we *do not see.*"

When it comes to faith in Jesus, not seeing is believing! When you believe in Jesus without seeing him with your eyes, you will please God and be rewarded for your faith. It's true—read Hebrews 11:6 for the details!

■ Something to Think About

Hebrews 11 is a list of heroes of faith from the Bible. Take the time to read it and be inspired by their examples of faith. By following their examples and believing in Jesus, you too can be a faith hero!

Dear Jesus,

I praise you for _____

_____

_____

I'm sorry for _____

_____

_____

I ask you for _____

_____

_____

I thank you for _____

_____

_____ Amen.

Heroes of Faith Word Search

ABEL
ABRAHAM
BARAK
GIDEON
JEPHTHAH
JOSEPH
NOAH
SAMSON
SAMUEL

A	L	E	U	M	A	S	N	J
G	B	R	V	A	O	O	E	J
I	M	E	R	Z	A	P	I	O
D	T	A	L	H	H	Q	K	S
E	L	R	H	T	R	M	A	E
O	N	S	H	A	U	D	R	P
N	H	A	Q	N	R	H	A	H
H	H	I	B	D	Y	B	B	M
S	A	M	S	O	N	W	A	C

■ **Theme for the Week: Faith**

■ **Key Verse for the Week**
Believe in the Lord Jesus, and you will be saved—you and your household.
—Acts 16:31

■ **Bible Reading: 1 Kings 17:7-16**

You Want Me to Do *What?*

The widow in today's Bible passage was down to her last handful of flour and a few drops of oil. Her cupboards were empty. She was preparing her last meal for herself and her son. Her stomach must have been growling with hunger when Elijah asked her to stop and give him some food first.

Elijah told her, "The jar of flour will not be used up and the jug of oil will not run dry until the day the Lord gives rain on the land" (1 Kings 17:14).

The widow's faith was put to the test. She had a clear choice to make. Which did she choose?

_____ 1. No faith: Her son was so hungry! She said, "You want me to do *what?* No, Elijah, I can't give you any food. I don't believe God can keep my jars from running out of flour and oil."

_____ 2. Faith: The widow believed and obeyed God. She went home, made a small cake of bread for Elijah, and then fed her family.

Although the widow was afraid, she wisely chose to obey by faith. She put her faith in God, who kept the promise. Her oil and flour never ran out until it rained again! And after it rained, the food started to grow again and God continued to provide for her family.

■ **Something to Think About**
When God tells you to love your enemies and pray for those who persecute you, have you ever said, "You want me to do *what?*" You need faith like the widow's to obey God's word!

Dear Jesus,

I praise you for _____

_____

_____

I'm sorry for _____

_____

_____

I ask you for _____

_____

_____

I thank you for _____

_____

_____ *Amen.*

Breadsticks

What You Need
Refrigerated breadsticks (package
of 8)
Cookie sheet
Pizza sauce (optional)

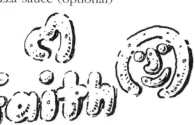

How to Do It
1. Open the package and separate the breadsticks.
2. On an ungreased cookie sheet use five breadsticks to form letters that spell out the word *faith*.
3. Form another breadstick into a circle (the head), and cut another to form into eyes, ears, nose, and a mouth (faith needs head knowledge—knowing who Jesus is).
4. Form the last breadstick into a heart (faith needs the heart—trusting that Jesus saved you).
5. Bake according to package directions.
6. Share the breadsticks with others and tell them about the widow's faith. Serve with pizza sauce, if you like.

■ Theme for the Week: Faith

■ Key Verse for the Week

Believe in the Lord Jesus, and you will be saved—you and your household.

—Acts 16:31

■ Bible Reading: Ephesians 2:8-10

But . . . I'm a Good Kid!

My name is Judy. I don't listen to my mom or dad. I fight with my brothers and sisters, and I only go to church because my parents make me.

My name is Jordana. I try to obey my mom and dad and share with my brothers and sisters. I also read my Bible and pray every day.

Who's the good kid here? Is it Judy or Jordana? (Not too tough to figure this one out, is it?) Pretty obvious the answer is Jordana.

Now here's another question for you. Which kid is good enough to go to heaven? If you answered Judy—you're wrong. If you answered Jordana—you're wrong again! When it comes to going to heaven, God doesn't look at how good or bad you've been. God cares about one thing: Do you believe in Jesus Christ?

Although God wants you to be a good kid, getting to heaven can only happen through faith in Jesus. "For it is by grace you have been saved, through faith—and this not from yourselves, it is the gift of God—not by works, so that no one can boast" (Ephesians 2:8-9).

So by all means, be a good kid. Just don't think that's what will get you into heaven!

■ Something to Think About

If going to heaven depends only on faith in Jesus, why should you try to be good? The answer is simple. If you love Jesus and have faith, you'll *want* to be good!

Dear Jesus,

I praise you for _____

_____

_____

I'm sorry for _____

_____

_____

I ask you for _____

_____

_____

I thank you for _____

_____

_____ Amen.

Decode the Faith Message

φ ο ρ   ι τ   ι σ   β ψ   γ ρ α χ ε   ψ ο υ   η α ϖ ε

β ε ε ν   σ α ϖ ε δ   τ η ρ ο υ γ η   φ α ι τ η!

(Ephesians 2:8a)

Key				
A = α	**G** = γ	**L** = λ	**Q** = θ	**V** = ϖ
B = β	**H** = η	**M** = μ	**R** = ρ	**W** = ω
C = χ	**I** = ι	**N** = ν	**S** = σ	**X** = Ξ
D = δ	**J** = φ	**O** = o	**T** = τ	**Y** = ψ
E = ε	**K** = κ	**P** = π	**U** = υ	**Z** = ζ
F = φ				

■ Theme for the Week: Faith

■ Key Verse for the Week

Believe in the Lord Jesus, and you will be saved—you and your household.

—*Acts 16:31*

■ Bible Reading: 1 Corinthians 13:1-3

Milk and Cookies

Think of some things that just have to go together—you can't have one without the other. Here are a few to get you started:

- Peanut butter and jelly
- Toothbrush and toothpaste
- Milk and cookies
- Pencil and eraser

What good is a pair of water skis without a boat to pull you? A tennis racket is useless without a tennis ball. It's also very difficult to play on a teeter-totter without a friend on the other end!

The Bible says that faith without love is worthless. It's as useless as a kite without wind. First Corinthians 13:2 puts it this way: "If I have a faith that can move mountains, but have not love, I am nothing."

Some people like milk and cookies together and some people don't. But when it comes to faith and love belonging together, God gives no options. The God who is love says you can't have real faith without love too.

■ Something to Think About

Invite a friend or cousin over for milk and cookies. Tell him or her what you learned today about faith and love.

Dear Jesus,

I praise you for _____

_____

_____

I'm sorry for _____

_____

_____

I ask you for _____

_____

_____

I thank you for _____

_____

_____ Amen.

Chocolate Chip Cookies

(A Large but Delicious Batch)
What You Need

3 eggs
2⅔ cups (.64 L) brown sugar
1½ cups (.36 L) sugar
2 cups (.48 L) butter, softened
2 tablespoons (30 mL) vanilla
6 cups (1.44 L) presifted flour
1½ teaspoons (7.5 mL) salt
1½ teaspoons (7.5 mL) baking soda
2 packages chocolate chips

How to Do It
1. Ask an adult to help you in the kitchen.
2. Preheat oven to 350°.
3. In a large bowl, beat eggs 4-5 minutes. Add sugars, vanilla, and butter, mixing thoroughly to combine. In a separate bowl, combine flour, salt, and baking soda. Add to egg mixture. Stir in chocolate chips. Drop batter by tablespoon onto baking sheet.
4. Bake 12-15 minutes. Cool ten minutes before removing from sheet.

■ Theme for the Week: Faith

■ Key Verse for the Week

Believe in the Lord Jesus, and you will be saved—you and your household.

—*Acts 16:31*

■ Bible Reading: 1 Corinthians 16:13-14; 2 Corinthians 1:24

Stand Firm!

When Paul—the writer of 1 and 2 Corinthians—tells you to stand firm, he's not talking about staying away from quicksand or standing in one spot all day. He wants you to stand firm in your faith: "Be on your guard; stand firm in the faith" (1 Corinthians 16:13).

How can you stand firm in your faith? It goes back to what you learned this week about your head and heart!

Knowing that Jesus is real involves your *head*. In order to know more about Jesus you need to read your Bible and learn from Christian parents, teachers, and pastors. You can also learn from Christian books and music.

Believing God saved you involves your *heart*. To keep your believing heart strong, spend regular time in prayer. Thank Jesus for saving you and share your love for him with others.

Don't trip, stumble, or sink away in your faith. By learning more about Jesus and believing in him, you'll be able to stand firm in your faith!

■ Something to Think About

Luke 6:46-49 tells about a foolish man who builds his house on the sand and a wise man who builds his house on the rock. Read the Bible passage and find out whose house was able to stand firm!

Dear Jesus,

I praise you for _____

_____

_____

I'm sorry for _____

_____

_____

I ask you for _____

_____

_____

I thank you for _____

_____

_____ Amen.

Toothpick Tower
Can you meet the toothpick tower challenge?

What You Need
Box of toothpicks

How to Do It
1. Place two toothpicks side by side, about one inch apart.
2. Place the next two on top of the first toothpicks in the other direction. (If you're playing with a partner, take turns laying toothpicks.)
3. See how many toothpicks you can use before your tower topples! (If you're playing with a partner, the last person to add two toothpicks wins.)

■ Theme for the Week: Faith

■ Key Versc for the Week

Write the key verse for the week on the lines below.

_____

_____

_____

—*Acts 16:31*

■ This Week I Learned . . .

Sunday
Faith has to do with my head—knowing Jesus—and my heart—believing in him (Acts 16:25-31).

Monday
Faith is knowing and believing in Jesus even when I can't see him with my eyes (Hebrews 11:1, 6).

Tuesday
I need to obey God in faith just like the widow did when Elijah asked her for bread (1 Kings 17:7-16).

Wednesday
Being a good kid won't get me to heaven. The only way I'll be able to live with Jesus forever is by believing in him (Ephesians 2:8-10).

Thursday
Some things just can't be separated. The Bible says that my faith without love is nothing (1 Corinthians 13:1-3).

Friday
In order to stand firm in my faith, I need to make a habit of reading the Bible and praying (1 Corinthians 16:13-14; 2 Corinthians 1:24).

■ Something to Think About

What's the most important thing you learned this week about faith?

_____

_____

_____

Dear Jesus,

I praise you for _____
_____
_____

I'm sorry for _____
_____
_____

I ask you for _____
_____
_____

I thank you for _____
_____
_____ Amen.

Flannelboard Stories

What You Need

2' x 3' (60 cm x 90 cm) piece of cardboard

Glue

Plain white or light-blue flannel to cover the cardboard and for the back of the figures

Magazines, catalogs, and church school papers

How to Do It

1. Cover the cardboard with flannel and glue in place.
2. Pick a Bible story that you want to tell with your flannelboard (for example, The Wise and Foolish Builders, Luke 6:46-49).
3. Decide which people or things need to be in your story and cut them out of the magazines, catalogs, and church school papers.
4. Glue flannel to the back of the figures you cut out.
5. Practice telling the story on your flannelboard.
6. Share your faith by telling the story to neighborhood kids, your family and friends, or at a local daycare center.

■ **Theme for the Week: Honesty**

■ **Key Versc for the Week**

The LORD detests lying lips, but he delights in men who are truthful.

—Proverbs 12:22

■ **Bible Reading: Proverbs 12:22; Proverbs 14:5, 25**

Nothing but the Truth

If you are ever called as a witness in a court of law, you'll be asked this question: Do you swear to tell the truth, the whole truth, and nothing but the truth? In other words, Do you promise to be honest?

This week's key verse, Proverbs 12:22, says, "The LORD detests lying lips, but he delights in men who are truthful." In other words, God not only wants your words to be honest, but also your actions. When you help a friend cheat on her homework, your actions are dishonest. When you sneak an extra cookie out of the kitchen after your mom said no, your actions are deceitful.

Proverbs 14:5 and 25 both mention deceit, which is the opposite of honesty. Deceit is when you trick someone or mislead them. It's hard to trust someone who plays tricks on you all the time because you never know when she's telling the truth.

God loves honesty. When you show by your actions that you are an honest person, your friends will trust you with their secrets and your parents will trust what you say and do. And most importantly, your honest words and actions will delight the Lord!

■ **Something to Think About**

Here's a good motto for the week:

Honesty only! Never exaggerate or stretch the truth about yourself.

Write down the underlined letters:

_____

Make the word part of your character!

Guess What, Jesus?

Dear Jesus,

I praise you for _____
_____
_____

I'm sorry for _____
_____
_____

I ask you for _____
_____
_____

I thank you for _____
_____
_____ Amen.

Word Puzzle

Below each line is a letter in the alphabet. Write the letter that comes before it in the blank.

"<u>J</u> <u>O</u> <u>T</u> <u>U</u> <u>F</u> <u>B</u> <u>E</u>' <u>T</u> <u>Q</u> <u>F</u> <u>B</u> <u>L</u> <u>J</u> <u>O</u> <u>H</u> <u>U</u> <u>I</u> <u>F</u>

<u>U</u> <u>S</u> <u>V</u> <u>U</u> <u>I</u> <u>J</u> <u>O</u> <u>M</u> <u>P</u> <u>W</u> <u>F</u>' <u>X</u> <u>F</u> <u>X</u> <u>J</u> <u>M</u> <u>M</u> <u>J</u> <u>O</u>

<u>B</u> <u>M</u> <u>M</u> <u>U</u> <u>I</u> <u>J</u> <u>O</u> <u>H</u> <u>T</u> <u>H</u> <u>S</u> <u>P</u> <u>X</u> <u>V</u> <u>Q</u> <u>J</u> <u>O</u> <u>U</u> <u>P</u>

<u>I</u> <u>J</u> <u>N</u> <u>X</u> <u>I</u> <u>P</u> <u>J</u> <u>T</u> <u>U</u> <u>I</u> <u>F</u> <u>I</u> <u>F</u> <u>B</u> <u>E</u>' <u>U</u> <u>I</u> <u>B</u> <u>U</u>

<u>J</u> <u>T</u> <u>D</u> <u>I</u> <u>S</u> <u>J</u> <u>T</u> <u>U</u>." <u>F</u> <u>Q</u> <u>I</u> <u>F</u> <u>T</u> <u>J</u> <u>B</u> <u>O</u> <u>T</u> 4:15.

■ **Theme for the Week: Honesty**

■ **Key Verse for the Week**

The LORD detests lying lips, but he delights in men who are truthful.
—*Proverbs 12:22*

■ **Bible Reading: Genesis 12:10-20**

Little White Lies

When they were entering Egypt, Abram told his wife, Sarai, to tell everyone that he was her brother. Abram knew the men of Egypt would see how beautiful Sarai was and would want to kill him so they could marry her.

After all, it wasn't a big lie, since Abram really was Sarai's stepbrother (Genesis 20:12). Abram told a little lie because he wanted to save his life. He figured God didn't care much about little white lies.

Sure enough, when Pharaoh saw beautiful Sarai, he took her to be his wife. God watched over Sarai by making Pharaoh and his family terribly sick. When Pharaoh dis-

covered the truth, he asked Abram, "Why didn't you tell me she was your wife? Why did you say, 'She is my sister,' so that I took her to be my wife?" (Genesis 12:18-19). Pharaoh was angry that Abram had lied.

Sometimes telling a little white lie instead of telling the truth and being punished seems like an easy escape from trouble. But God didn't like little white lies in Abram's time, and God doesn't like little white lies today. Here's a rhyme to help you remember that God loves honesty.

> *Whether your lie is big or small,*
> *God loves truth most of all!*

■ **Something to Think About**

Abram was slow to learn his lesson. He repeated the same lie when he met King Abimelech! Read Genesis 20 for the details.

Dear Jesus,

I praise you for _____

_____

_____

I'm sorry for _____

_____

_____

I ask you for _____

_____

_____

I thank you for _____

_____

_____ Amen.

Sweet Potato Plant

Give this fun project a try and watch the plant grow instead of a lie!

What You Need

Sweet potato with roots that look like whiskers, Toothpicks, Glass, Water

How to Do It

1. Poke four toothpicks around the middle of the sweet potato (see illustration).
2. Place the potato in a tall clear glass filled with water (the toothpicks should rest on the rim of your glass).
3. Keep the top half of the sweet potato dry and the bottom half covered in water. Keep adding water to the roots when needed.
4. In six to eight days, the roots will begin to grow on the bottom of the potato and green leaves will start to grow from the top of the potato.
5. After a few weeks the vine will be big! Fill a large pot with dirt and plant your sweet potato root-side down.

■ **Theme for the Week: Honesty**

■ **Key Verse for the Week**

The LORD detests lying lips, but he delights in men who are truthful.

—Proverbs 12:22

■ **Bible Reading: Psalm 119:29-32**

Honesty Is the Only Policy

You've probably heard the motto "Honesty is the best policy." Although that's a good rule, Christians need to live by a better one. With God, honesty is not the best policy, it's the *only* policy!

It's hard to tell the truth all the time, isn't it? One of the ways you can help yourself choose honesty instead of lies is by following the example of the writer of Psalm 119. Here's what you, like the psalmist, can do:

- Ask God for help. The psalmist prays that God will help him be honest: "Keep me from deceitful ways; be gracious to me through your law" (verse 29). He needs God's help to stay out of places and conversations that would cause him to be dishonest.

- Keep God's Word in your heart. The psalmist says, "I have chosen the way of truth; I have set my heart on your laws" (verse 30). The best way to keep your heart on God's laws is by memorizing Bible verses. Search for verses that teach about honesty. When you read your Bible every day, God's Word will help you choose the way of truth too.

■ **Something to Think About**

Follow the psalmist's example in your prayers today. Ask God for help in making honesty your best and only policy.

Dear Jesus,

I praise you for _____
_____
_____

I'm sorry for _____
_____
_____

I ask you for _____
_____
_____

I thank you for _____
_____
_____ *Amen.*

Finish the Phrases

Before you read today's devotional, had you ever heard the motto "Honesty is the best policy"? Put your thinking cap on and see if you can figure out the endings to the following phrases.

1. A stitch in time saves _____.

2. Don't count your chickens before they're _____.

3. A penny saved is a penny _____.

4. Birds of a feather flock _____.

5. Don't cry over spilled _____.

■ Theme for the Week: Honesty

■ Kcy Verse for the Week

The LORD detests lying lips, but he delights in men who are truthful.

—*Proverbs 12:22*

■ Bible Reading: Acts 5:1-11

They Died When They Lied

Ananias and Sapphira lied when they pretended to give Peter all of the money they received when they sold some of their land. When Ananias gave the money to the apostles, Peter said to him, "You have not lied to men but to God" (Acts 5:4). Did you read what happened next? When Peter quit speaking, Ananias fell down and died!

Three hours later, Ananias's wife Sapphira came to the apostles. "Peter asked her, 'Tell me, is this the price you and Ananias got for the land?'"(Acts 5:8). When she said yes, Sapphira fell down and died!

We can be thankful that God doesn't usually strike people dead when they disobey God by lying. Even though this Bible story took place years ago, it is still a powerful lesson of how much God hates lies.

Have you cvcr acted like Ananias and Sapphira by trying to hide the truth from your parents, friends, or teachers? Some lies can be hidden for a short time and some lies are never discovered. You may be able to hide your lies from other people, but it is impossible to hide your lies from God, who knows all things!

■ Something to Think About

Are you hiding the truth from someone? If so, tell her the truth today. Remember, you can't hide your lies from God!

Dear Jesus,

I praise you for _____

_____

_____

I'm sorry for _____

_____

_____

I ask you for _____

_____

_____

I thank you for _____

_____

_____ Amen.

Mozzarella Puffs (10 servings)

Serve these to your family or friends, and tell them what you've learned about hiding the truth.

What You Need

1 tube refrigerated biscuits (7½ ounces)
1 teaspoon (5 mL) dried oregano
2-3 ounces (56-84 g) mozzarella cheese (not grated)
2 tablespoons (30 mL) pizza sauce
Baking sheet

How to Do It

1. Ask an adult to help you in the kitchen.
2. Indent the center of each biscuit.
3. Sprinkle with oregano.
4. Cut the mozzarella into ten cubes.
5. Place a cheese cube in the center of each biscuit.
6. Seal the cheese by pinching the dough tightly around it.
7. Place seam side down on an ungreased baking sheet.
8. Spread pizza sauce over tops.
9. Bake at 375° for 10-12 minutes or until golden brown.

—*Taste of Home*, July/August 1996.
Reprinted with permission from *Taste of Home* magazine,
P.O. Box 992, Greendale WI 53129.

W E E K **8** E I G H T T H U R S D A Y _____

■ Theme for the Week: Honesty

■ Key Verse for the Week
The LORD detests lying lips, but he delights in men who are truthful.

—Proverbs 12:22

■ Bible Reading: Proverbs 12:17-22

Lies and Bubbles

Have you ever blown bubbles and watched them float in the air? How long do they usually last? Most bubbles pop within a few seconds and disappear.

In that sense, telling lies is a lot like popping bubbles. Proverbs 12:19 says, "Truthful lips endure forever, but a lying tongue lasts only a moment."

People don't usually trust someone who is known to lie or exaggerate the truth. Such a person's stories are like bubbles popping in the air. People listen to the person's words but don't believe anything she says. Conversations vanish and pop like bubbles into thin air if there's no truth to hold them together and give them meaning.

A lie may last only a moment, but the hurt and pain it can cause others can last a lifetime!

The Bible says that truth, on the other hand, lasts forever. You will make lifetime friends if you are known to be truthful and honest. More importantly, God will delight in you for telling the truth. (Read the theme verse again!)

■ Something to Think About

Think about the last time you talked with your best friend. Did your words last only a moment (like bubbles)? Or will they endure forever?

Dear Jesus,

I praise you for _____

_____

_____

I'm sorry for _____

_____

_____

I ask you for _____

_____

_____

I thank you for _____

_____

_____ Amen.

Bubble Recipe

What You Need

1 cup (.24 L) Joy liquid dish soap
2 (.48 L) cups warm water
4 tablespoons glycerine (found in most drugstores)
Ice cream pail or bucket
Various items to be used as bubble blowers—straws, a hanger bent into a circle, biscuit cutters . . . use your imagination!

How to Do It

1. Mix ingredients in a clean ice cream pail or bucket.
2. Dip the bubble blowers into the mixture and blow them in the air.
3. Ask your family, friends, or neighbors to join you. Tell them what you learned today about lies and bubbles.

■ Theme for the Week: Honesty

■ Key Verse for the Week

The LORD detests lying lips, but he delights in men who are truthful.

—Proverbs 12:22

■ Bible Reading: Genesis 4:1-9

"I Don't Know"

Has your mom or dad ever asked you and your brothers and sisters, "Who threw a candy wrapper behind the couch?" Or "Who left the closet door open again?" And did everybody answer at the same time, "I don't know"?

In today's Bible story, two brothers, Cain and Abel, brought their offerings to the Lord. "The LORD looked with favor on Abel and his offering, but on Cain and his offering he did not look with favor" (Genesis 4:4-5). This made Cain very angry. He was so filled with jealousy that he brought Abel out to a field and killed him.

"Then the LORD said to Cain, 'Where is your brother Abel?' 'I don't know,' he replied. 'Am I my brother's keeper?'" (Genesis 4:9).

Cain disobeyed and hurt God twice—first by murdering his brother, second by telling a lie. Have you ever lied and said, "I don't know" to stay out of trouble? Remember that lying to God only doubles your troubles.

■ Something to Think About

You may fool people with "I don't know" once in awhile, but you can never fool God. God knows everything!

Dear Jesus,

I praise you for _____

_____

_____

I'm sorry for _____

_____

_____

I ask you for _____

_____

_____

I thank you for _____

_____

_____ Amen.

Tongue Twisters

Although lying leads lips to lots of trouble, these tongue twisters will only tangle your tongue! Give them a try!

Sheila Shorter sought a suitor;
Sheila sought a suitor short.
Sheila's suitor's sure to suit her;
Short's the suitor Sheila sought!

A tutor who tooted a flute,
tried to teach two tooters to toot.
Said the two to the tutor,
"Is it harder to toot,
or tutor two tooters to toot?"

Six thick thistle sticks.

Ellen's elegant elephant.

—*Tongue Twisters* by Charles Keller, Simon & Schuster, Inc., 1989.

W E E K **8** E I G H T S A T U R D A Y _____
(DATE)

■ Theme for the Week: Honesty

■ Key Verse for the Week

Write the key verse for the week on the lines below.

_____

_____

_____

—*Proverbs 12:22*

■ This Week I Learned . . .

Sunday
God will delight in me when my words and actions are honest and true (Proverbs 12:22; Proverbs 14:5, 25).

Monday
Whether my lie is big or small, God desires truth most of all! (Genesis 12:10-20).

Tuesday
I need to pray for God's help and keep God's law in my heart in order to choose honesty as the only policy in my life (Psalm 119:29-32).

Wednesday
The story of Ananias and Sapphira shows how serious God is about people not lying. They died when they lied! (Acts 5:1-11).

Thursday
Although lies last only a moment (like bubbles), the hurt and pain lies cause can sometimes last a lifetime (Proverbs 12:17-22).

Friday
When I lie and say "I don't know," my troubles double. God knows everything! (Genesis 4:1-9).

■ Something to Think About

What did you learn about honesty and lies this week?

_____

_____

_____

_____

Dear Jesus,

I praise you for _____

_____

_____

I'm sorry for _____

_____

_____

I ask you for _____

_____

_____

I thank you for _____

_____

_____ Amen.

Proverbs Puzzles

Cross out the letter "P" in the puzzles and you'll discover what Proverbs says about honesty.

PAPTPRPUPTPHPFPUPLPWPIPTPNPEPSPSPGPIPVPEPSPHPOPNPEPSPTPT-
PEPSPTPIPMPOPN PYP,BPUPTPAPFPAPLPSPEPWPIPTPNPEPSPSPTPEPLPLP-
SPLPIPEPSP.

—Proverbs 12:17

PBPUPYPTPHPEPTPRPUPTPHPAPNPDPDPOPNPOPTPSPEPLPLPIPTP.

—Proverbs 23:23a

■ Theme for the Week: Love

■ Kcy Verse for the Week

Love the Lord your God with all your heart and with all your soul and with all your mind. This is the first and greatest commandment. And the second is like it: Love your neighbor as yourself.

—Matthew 22:37-39

■ Bible Reading: 1 Corinthians 13:4-7, 13

It's the Greatest!

First Corinthians 13 is the Bible's "love chapter." To find out what love is, fill in the blanks below. You'll find the answers in 1 Corinthians 13:4-7.

Love is _____, love is _____. It does not envy, it does not boast, it is not proud. It is not rude, it is not self-seeking, it is not easily angered, it keeps no record of wrongs. Love does not delight in evil but rejoices with the truth. It always _____, always _____, always _____, always _____.

That's quite a list, isn't it? Love is so much more than hugs or kisses. It's more than the words you say. Love is especially the things you do. So, even though telling your dad and mom that you love them is a wonderful thing to do, your parents will *really* know that you love them by the way you act. Did you obey them today? Were you kind to your pets? Did you fight with your brother or sister? True love pours out of your heart and into your words and actions.

■ Something to Think About

The Bible says that one of these three is "the greatest." Which of these do you think it is?

_____ Faith   _____Hope   _____Love

(You'll find the answer in 1 Corinthians 13:13.)

Dear Jesus,

I praise you for _____

_____

_____

I'm sorry for _____

_____

_____

I ask you for _____

_____

_____

I thank you for _____

_____

_____ Amen.

Shining Lights

For this week's devotions, ask your dad or mom to help you hang a string of Christmas lights in your prayer closet. If you don't have Christmas lights, use a night light, flashlight, or small lamp when you have your time of prayer and Bible reading.

God's love needs to shine in my heart, like a light that shines in the dark!

■ Theme for the Week: Love

■ Key Versc for the Week

Love the Lord your God with all your heart and with all your soul and with all your mind. This is the first and greatest commandment. And the second is like it: Love your neighbor as yourself.

—*Matthew 22:37-39*

■ Bible Reading: Psalm 103:11; John 3:16

The World's Greatest Gift

Think about the best present you ever received. Was it a bike, a radio, or some toy you'd been wanting badly for a long time? Was it all wrapped up on the table when you woke up on your birthday, or was it hidden away somewhere? Do you remember how you felt when you got it?

Unlike your favorite present, the world's greatest gift wasn't bought in a store. You didn't get it wrapped in a pretty package with a bow.

The greatest gift you could ever receive comes from God. "For God so loved the world that he gave his one and only Son, that whoever believes in him shall not perish but have eternal life" (John 3:16). What a present! God gave you the gift of Jesus because he loves you so much!

This present was very expensive. It cost Jesus his life. When Jesus came to earth he was made fun of, beaten, and put on a cross to die. Why would God let that happen to his precious Son? Because God loves you deeply. God sent Jesus so that your sins could be forgiven.

That's love! To receive this gift, you must do one thing. You need to believe in your heart that Jesus died for your sins. If you believe in Jesus, you'll live with him forever in heaven.

■ Something to Think About

God's love is as _____ as the heavens are above the earth! Read Psalm 103:11 and fill in the unbelievable answer.

Dear Jesus,

I praise you for _____

_____

_____

I'm sorry for _____

_____

_____

I ask you for _____

_____

_____

I thank you for _____

_____

_____ Amen.

Tin Can Candles

Use your candle as a reminder of God's gift of love during your time of Bible reading and prayer. Or set it on the table to use during family devotions.

What You Need
Clean empty soup can
Hammer and nail
Glue
Ribbon or lace (optional)
Votive candle

How to Do It
1. Fill the can with water and freeze.
2. Make a heart pattern (see illustration) and tape it on the side of the can.
3. Use a hammer and nail to punch holes in the can along the lines of your pattern.
4. Let the ice melt, pour out the water, and carefully dry the can.
5. Glue ribbon or lace on the top and bottom edges of the can, if you like.
6. Set the candle in the can. The flame will shine through the nail holes.

■ Theme for the Week: Love

■ Key Verse for the Week

Love the Lord your God with all your heart and with all your soul and with all your mind. This is the first and greatest commandment. And the second is like it: Love your neighbor as yourself.
—*Matthew 22:37-39*

■ Bible Reading: Matthew 22:34-39

The Greatest Rule

What's the greatest rule or commandment?

a. _____ You shall not steal.

b. _____ Honor your father and mother.

c. _____ Love the Lord your God with all your heart, soul, and mind.

d. _____ Remember the Sabbath day by keeping it holy.

If you picked "c," you're right! In Matthew 22:37-38 Jesus says, "Love the Lord your God with all your heart and with all your soul and with all your mind. This is the first and greatest commandment. And the second is like it: Love your neighbor as yourself."

God wants to be the number one love of your life. God wants you to love him with all your *heart, soul, mind . . . your whole being!*

That means everything you say, think, and do should shout, "I love God!"

■ Something to Think About

Remember when you used to have show-and-tell at school? Have show-and-tell with God today. Show God through your actions and tell God in your prayers how much you love him!

Dear Jesus,

I praise you for _____
_____
_____

I'm sorry for _____
_____
_____

I ask you for _____
_____
_____

I thank you for _____
_____
_____ Amen.

Heart Pizzas

What You Need
Refrigerated biscuits
Pizza sauce
Cheese
Favorite pizza toppings
   (optional)
Cookie sheet

How to Do It
1. Ask an adult for permission to work in the kitchen.
2. Roll out each biscuit.
3. Form each biscuit into a heart shape.
4. Put a small amount of pizza sauce on each biscuit and top with cheese.
5. Add other favorite pizza toppings, if you wish.
6. Put biscuits on greased cookie sheet. Bake at 450° for 8-10 minutes.
7. Share the pizzas with your family. Tell them what you learned today about God's love!

■ Theme for the Week: Love

■ Key Verse for the Week

Love the Lord your God with all your heart and with all your soul and with all your mind. This is the first and greatest commandment. And the second is like it: Love your neighbor as yourself.
—Matthew 22:37-39

■ Bible Reading: Matthew 5:43-48

The Greatest Example

List three people that you love:

_____

_____

_____

Some people (like the ones you listed) are very easy to love. It's simple to love the people who love you. Even people who don't know Jesus love the people who are nice to them. There's nothing hard about giving that kind of love.

It's tough to love people who don't like you. But that's exactly what Jesus tells us to do: "Love your enemies and pray for those who persecute you" (Matthew 5:44).

Love and pray for your enemies? Doesn't Jesus realize how nasty some of the boys in your class can be? Doesn't he know that one of the girls told lies about you? Does he really mean you have to love everyone?

Jesus does mean that. But keep in mind that there's a difference between *loving* someone and *liking* that person. You can't help how you feel about someone—but you can choose how you treat her. Even the people you love sometimes do things you don't like, but that doesn't stop you from loving them.

Jesus showed us what he meant by showing love to his enemies while he was on earth. Day after day, Jesus loved people no one else would talk to or even look at. Jesus, our greatest example, loved his enemies.

■ Something to Think About

If you're a daughter of your Father in heaven, you need to love and pray for everyone—including your enemies.

Dear Jesus,

I praise you for _____

_____

_____

I'm sorry for _____

_____

_____

I ask you for _____

_____

_____

I thank you for _____

_____

_____ Amen.

Decode the Verse

Decode the verse by changing each letter to the letter that comes before it in the alphabet.

"But I tell you:

M P W F • Z P V S • F O F N J F T, • E P • H P P E •

___ ___ ___ ___   ___ ___ ___ ___   ___ ___ ___ ___ ___ ___ ___,   ___ ___   ___ ___ ___ ___ •

U P • U I P T F • X I P • I B U F • Z P V.

___ ___   ___ ___ ___ ___ ___   ___ ___ ___   ___ ___ ___ ___   ___ ___ ___."

—Luke 6:27

■ Theme for the Week: Love

■ Key Verse for the Week

Love the Lord your God with all your heart and with all your soul and with all your mind. This is the first and greatest commandment. And the second is like it: Love your neighbor as yourself.
—Matthew 22:37-39

■ Bible Reading: Luke 10:29-37

The Greatest Neighbor

A man asked Jesus, "Who is my neighbor?" Jesus answered by telling him a story called "The Parable of the Good Samaritan" (Luke 10:29-37).

One day a man was walking between two towns when a group of robbers stole from him, beat him, and left him half dead.

A priest (or pastor) was walking down the road and saw the injured man. Instead of helping him, he went to the other side of the road. A little later, a Levite (an important church leader) walked down the same road.

When he saw the man, he went to the other side of the road too. Then a Samaritan came down the road. No one liked Samaritans or thought they were as good as priests and Levites. But the Samaritan went to the man lying along the road. He picked him up and took care of him.

Which of the three, asked Jesus, was a neighbor to the man who fell into the hands of robbers? The priest and Levite probably gave sermons and lessons on loving others, but did they listen to their own lessons? It was the Samaritan who showed the man true love by helping and caring for him.

Even though he was from a different country, he was the greatest neighbor!

■ Something to Think About

Who are your neighbors? Is it the people who live next door or the ones who go to your church or school? Remember that Jesus wants you to love everyone, not just the people on your street, in your state or province, or even in your country!

Dear Jesus,

I praise you for _____

_____

_____

I'm sorry for _____

_____

_____

I ask you for _____

_____

_____

I thank you for _____

_____

_____ Amen.

Be a Great Neighbor!

Pick one of the following activities to show love to a person who is sick, sad, or lonely:

- If the person is new in town, invite her to come to your house and play.
- Make and mail her a special card. Put a piece of candy, stick of gum, or a few stickers in the envelope too.
- If she goes to your school, ask her if she'd like to play with you at recess.
- Tell her something that you really like about her.

■ Theme for the Week: Love

■ Kcy Verse for the Week

Love the Lord your God with all your heart and with all your soul and with all your mind. This is the first and greatest commandment. And the second is like it: Love your neighbor as yourself.
—Matthew 22:37-39

■ Bible Reading: John 13:34-35

The Greatest Sign

Question: When you see a person wearing a uniform and directing traffic, what do you think that person's job is?

Answer: A police officer.

Question: When you see a person standing in front of a classroom and helping students, what is that person's job?

Answer: A teacher.

Question: When you see a person with a heart full of love for God and for other people, what do you call that person?

Answer: A Christian.

The answers to those questions are pretty obvious, aren't they? The signs are clear. Police officers wear uniforms and direct traffic. Teachers write on chalkboards and help students. Followers of Jesus love one another. The sign that shows everyone that you belong to Jesus is love. Jesus says, "All men will know that you are my disciples, if you love one another" (John 13:35).

You don't have to stand on the street corner and shout that you're a follower of Jesus. People will know you're a Christian by your love.

■ Something to Think About

Did you show others today, through your love, that you're a Christian? Ask Jesus to help you show others the sign that you belong to him by the way you treat them.

Dear Jesus,

I praise you for _____

_____

_____

I'm sorry for _____

_____

_____

I ask you for _____

_____

_____

I thank you for _____

_____

_____ Amen.

Love Messages

Sometime today, surprise each person in your family with a love message. Hide the messages in places where you know they'll be found. (Need some ideas? For your parents, in a favorite coffee mug or purse or briefcase; for your brothers or sisters, in their tennis shoes or on their pillows.)

What You Need
Pencil
Scissors
Paper

How to Do It
1. On the paper, draw one heart for each member of your family.
2. Cut out the hearts.
3. On each heart, write a message telling the person why you love him or her.

■ Theme for the Week: Love

■ Kcy Verse for the Week

Write the key verse for the week on the lines below.

_____

_____

_____

_____

_____

—Matthew 22:37-39

■ This Week I Learned . . .

Sunday
Love is the greatest and most important thing to God. It is shown through words and actions (1 Corinthians 13:4-7, 13).

Monday
God loved me so much that he gave me Jesus, the greatest gift I will ever receive (Psalm 103:11; John 3:16).

Tuesday

The greatest rule is to love God first. I should love God with my whole being—heart, soul, and mind (Matthew 22:34-39).

Wednesday
Jesus wants me to love my enemies. He is the greatest example of how to love those who are hard to love (Matthew 5:43-48).

Thursday
The greatest neighbors are the people who show love to everyone, no matter where they live or who they are (Luke 10:29-37).

Friday
The greatest sign that lets people see that I'm a Christian is love. Jesus' followers must love one another (John 13:34-35).

■ Something to Think About

Who did you show Jesus' love to this week?

Dear Jesus,

I praise you for _____
_____
_____

I'm sorry for _____
_____
_____

I ask you for _____
_____
_____

I thank you for _____
_____
_____ Amen.

Peanut Butter Brownie Cups

Show Jesus' love by sharing these special cupcakes with someone!

What You Need
1 package (21½ oz.) fudge brownie mix
15-18 miniature peanut butter cups
Paper cupcake liners

How to Do It
1. Ask an adult for permission before working in the kitchen.
2. Mix brownie batter according to package directions.
3. Fill paper-lined muffin cups ⅔ full.
4. Remove wrappers from peanut butter cups. Set one in each muffin cup.
5. Press down candy until the batter meets the top edge.
6. Bake at 350° for 20-25 minutes.

■ Theme for the Week: Respect

■ Key Verse for the Wcck

Show proper respect to everyone: Love the brotherhood of believers, fear God, honor the king.

—*1 Peter 2:17*

■ Bible Reading: 1 Peter 2:17

More Than Mr. or Mrs.

What's your favorite teacher's name? Most kids show respect to their teachers by using the titles Mr., Mrs., or Miss in front of their teachers' last names.

But there's more to showing respect than just remembering to say Mr. or Mrs. This week's theme verse says "Show proper respect to everyone: Love the brotherhood of believers, fear God, honor the king" (1 Peter 2:17).

So how do you do that? Here are some examples of showing respect that go beyond Mr. or Mrs. . . .

- Show love to God's creation and all the people God made—even when they're different than you (show proper respect to evcryonc)!
- Don't read your sister's diary, even when she forgets to lock it (respect the brotherhood of believers).
- Honor God by never swearing (fear God).
- Obey the rules of your family, school, and country and those who make them (honor the king).

■ Something to Think About

This week's focus on respect goes hand in hand with last week's focus on love. If you really love God first in your life and love your neighbors second, you'll find it easier to show respect to everyone!

Guess What, Jesus?

Dear Jesus,

I praise you for _____
_____
_____

I'm sorry for _____
_____
_____

I ask you for _____
_____
_____

I thank you for _____
_____
_____

Amen.

Gooey Delights

What You Need

1 8-ounce tube refrigerated crescent rolls
8 large marshmallows
¼ cup (.06 L) butter (or margarine), melted
¼ cup (.06 L) sugar
1 tablespoon (15 mL) ground cinnamon

How to Do It

1. Ask an adult if you may work in the kitchen.
2. Separate crescent rolls into eight triangles. Mix sugar and cinnamon.
3. Dip each marshmallow into butter and then roll in cinnamon-sugar mixture.
4. Place marshmallow on a triangle and pinch the dough around it. Seal all edges.
5. Dip tops of dough into remaining butter and cinnamon-sugar mixture.
6. Place sugar side up in greased muffin cups.
7. Bake at 375° for 13-15 minutes. Serve while warm.

■ Theme for the Week: Respect

■ Key Verse for the Week

Show proper respect to everyone: Love the brotherhood of believers, fear God, honor the king.

—1 Peter 2:17

■ Bible Reading: Revelation 4:8-11

Holy, Holy, Holy

What do you do when you hear kids or adults use God's name as a swear word? Do you shut off the TV if you hear an actor or actress using God's name as a swear word? When people use God's name to swear, they are being disrespectful to our holy and awesome God.

In today's Bible passage you can read about how the creatures in heaven respect God. "Day and night they never stop saying, 'Holy, holy, holy is the Lord God Almighty, who was, and is, and is to come'" (Revelation 4:8). God deserves your respect and reverence.

How do you show respect for God? The Bible isn't only talking about the way you speak to God in your prayers. You show respect for your holy Creator by showing love and respect to the people, the world, and all the creatures God made.

Praying to God with reverence, singing songs of praise, and enjoying God's good gifts are other ways to show respect to God. Join the heavenly creatures today in respecting and worshiping the holy Lord God Almighty!

■ Something to Think About

Respecting God's name is serious business. Check out Exodus 20:7 for God's command concerning his holy name.

Dear Jesus,

I praise you for _____

_____

_____

I'm sorry for _____

_____

_____

I ask you for _____

_____

_____

I thank you for _____

_____

_____ Amen.

Respecting God's Creation

You can show respect for God's creation and creatures by doing one or more of these activities.

- Get a large grocery bag and take a walk. Gather up the plastic bottles, aluminum cans, or other garbage that you find outside. Recycle whatever materials you can.
- Ask an adult for some birdseed and take a nature walk. Scatter some for birds, squirrels, and other small creatures.
- Be a watch person in your home for saving electricity. If no one's in the room, shut off the lights, TV, radio, or other appliances that are not being used.
- Keep God's world clean by not littering on the ground or in the lakes.

Which activity did you choose? Talk to your family and invite them to join you in showing respect for God's creation.

■ Theme for the Week: Respect

■ Key Verse for thc Week
Show proper respect to everyone: Love the brotherhood of believers, fear God, honor the king.

—*1 Peter 2:17*

■ Bible Reading: Exodus 20:12; Leviticus 19:3

Guess What My Mom Did?
Has your mom (or dad) ever made a decision that you didn't agree with?

_____ yes _____ no

You probably checked yes since it's rare for two people to always agree on everything. Now here's a more important question. Take your time and be honest.

After you disagreed with the decision your mom (or dad) made, did you ever talk disrespectfully about her (or him)?

_____ yes _____ no

Here's something you should know. God cares when you shrug your shoulders with disgust and say, "Guess what my mom did this time?" In fact, God cares so much about your relationship with your parents that there are verses in the Bible just for kids and their moms and dads. Here are a couple of them:

- "Each of you must respect his mother and father. . . . I am the Lord your God" (Leviticus 19:3).
- "Honor your father and your mother, so that you may live long in the land the Lord your God is giving you" (Exodus 20:12).

Respecting God means respecting your parents too!

■ Something to Think About
Sometimes parents and children don't agree. That's OK as long as the discussions and disagreements are wrapped up in respect.

Dear Jesus,

I praise you for _____

_____

_____

I'm sorry for _____

_____

_____

I ask you for _____

_____

_____

I thank you for _____

_____

_____ Amen.

A Parent Card

What You Need

Construction paper
Markers or crayons
Your school picture or another photograph of you
Glue

How to Do It

1. Fold a sheet of construction paper in half to form a card.
2. Glue your picture on the front of the card.
3. Use your crayons or markers to draw a design around it.
4. On the inside of the card, write a note to your mom or dad, using one or more of these message ideas, or your own idea:
   - List three or more reasons why you like your mom or dad.
   - Write out Exodus 20:12 or Leviticus 19:3.
   - Tell them how much you love them!

■ Theme for the Week: Respect

■ Key Verse for the Week

Show proper respect to everyone: Love the brotherhood of believers, fear God, honor the king.

—*1 Peter 2:17*

■ Bible Reading: Leviticus 19:32; 1 Thessalonians 5:12

Respecting the Substitute

I have a confession to make. When I was in elementary school, my friends and I gave our substitute teachers a very hard time. The whole class would do things like pretend to cough and sneeze and blow our noses or else we would "accidentally" drop our pencils and books from our desks. We showed no respect for the substitute.

God must have been very disappointed at what went on in our classroom. We completely ignored God's rules about respecting substitute teachers and other adults in authority over us—rules like 1 Thessalonians 5:12-13: "Respect those who work hard among you, who are over you in the Lord and who admonish you. Hold them in the highest regard in love because of their work."

"Dropping" my book off my desk in order to irritate the substitute teacher was not showing the respect that God wanted.

God gives teachers, neighbors, grandparents, and church members a very important responsibility—to help you grow into a woman of God! In return, God wants you to give them something back—your respect.

■ Something to Think About

If your classmates are in the habit of mistreating substitute teachers, I challenge you to be the leader who shows respect!

Dear Jesus,

I praise you for _____

_____

_____

I'm sorry for _____

_____

_____

I ask you for _____

_____

_____

I thank you for _____

_____

_____ *Amen.*

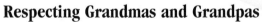

Respecting Grandmas and Grandpas

The Bible also talks about how we need to respect older people like your grandparents (read Leviticus 19:32). Enjoy one or more of the following activities with your grandpa, grandma, or favorite elderly friend.

- Go on a nature walk. Ask your grandparents to help you identify birds, flowers, and trees.
- Visit them at home, and bring along some flowers that you picked or cookies or muffins that you baked.
- Ask if you could interview them. Ahead of time, write a list of interview questions (like, What was your favorite toy when you were growing up? What was your school like? Who was president when you were my age?). Then use a tape recorder or video camera to record your interview.

■ Theme for the Week: Respect

■ Key Verse for the Week

Show proper respect to everyone: Love the brotherhood of believers, fear God, honor the king.

—1 Peter 2:17

■ Bible Reading: Ephesians 6:5; 1 Peter 2:17

I Pledge Allegiance

Does your teacher sometimes ask your class to stand up and say the Pledge of Allegiance? Together you face the flag, put your right hand over your heart, and say, "I pledge allegiance to the flag of the United States of America and to the Republic for which it stands, one nation, under God, indivisible, with liberty and justice for all."

No matter where you live, your country has its own traditions, songs, and flags to help people show respect to their country. Americans sing "The Star-Spangled Banner" and Canadians sing "O Canada."

Showing respect for your country is more than just a nice idea. It's God's plan for his people. First Peter 2:17 tells us to "show respect to everyone: Love the brotherhood of believers, fear God, honor the king."

Although you may not have a king ruling over your country, you do have a President or a Prime Minister or some other government official who makes laws to help you and the people in your country. The best way to show respect for these leaders is by remembering to pray for them each day.

■ Something to Think About

Write the name of your country's main leader:

_____

Say a prayer for him or her today!

Dear Jesus,

I praise you for _____
_____
_____

I'm sorry for _____
_____
_____

I ask you for _____
_____
_____

I thank you for _____
_____
_____ *Amen.*

Fruit Flag Pizza

What You Need
1 tube sugar cookie dough
4 ounces (112 g) whipping cream
8 ounces (224 g) cream cheese
½ cup (.12 L) sugar
Fruits that are the color of your flag:
 strawberries (red), blueberries
 (blue), kiwi (green), bananas
 (white), grapes (purple)
Cookie sheet

How to Do It
1. Ask an adult to help you in the kitchen.
2. Roll out cookie dough into the shape of a rectangle.
3. Place dough on cookie sheet and bake at 350° for 12 minutes. Cool.
4. Mix cream cheese, whipping cream, and sugar. Spread over crust.
5. Arrange the fruit to look like your country's flag.
6. Refrigerate until eaten.

■ Theme for the Week: Respect

■ Key Vcrsc for the Week

Show proper respect to everyone: Love the brotherhood of believers, fear God, honor the king.

—1 Peter 2:17

■ Bible Reading: 1 Thessalonians 4:11-12

I Get No Respect!

Have you ever been teased or had someone snoop through your desk? If that's happened to you, you probably got angry. Maybe you even complained and said, "I get no respect!"

Respect is a two-way deal. You give it and you receive it. This week you've been learning how to show respect to God, to God's creation, and to other people. Now it's time to think about how you can earn the respect of others.

Simply telling others, "You must respect me, or else!" will not be very effective. You may get a few laughs when you make this demand but probably very little respect.

First Thessalonians 4:11-12 has a better answer for earning the respect of others: "Make it your ambition to lead a quiet life, to mind your own business and to work with your hands, just as we told you, so that your daily life may win the respect of outsiders and so that you will not be dependent on anybody."

Every day (not just once in awhile) people are watching your actions and listening to your words. If they see and hear your love for the Lord, you will win their respect.

■ Something to Think About

Did you win the respect of others today? Ask God to help you win the respect of others in your daily life.

Dear Jesus,

I praise you for _____

_____

_____

I'm sorry for _____

_____

_____

I ask you for _____

_____

_____

I thank you for _____

_____

_____ Amen.

Respectable Word Search

Find the following words that your actions and conversations should contain if you want to win the respect of others.

CONSIDERATE   LOVING
CONTENT   OBEDIENT
FORGIVING   RESPECTFUL
GENEROUS   THANKFUL
JOYFUL   UNSELFISH
KIND

O	L	C	O	N	T	E	N	T	K	C
H	O	U	Z	E	J	P	Y	I	O	L
S	B	L	F	Q	E	I	N	N	T	U
I	E	O	W	T	B	D	S	J	Q	F
F	D	V	C	V	C	I	L	W	Y	K
L	I	I	Q	B	D	E	J	T	G	N
E	E	N	S	E	E	U	P	K	W	A
S	N	G	R	S	J	K	I	S	B	H
N	T	A	L	U	F	Y	O	J	E	T
U	T	S	U	O	R	E	N	E	G	R
E	F	O	R	G	I	V	I	N	G	B

■ Theme for the Week: Respect

■ Kcy Vcrse for the Week

Write the key verse for the week on the lines below.

_____

_____

_____

—1 Peter 2:17

■ This Week I Learned . . .

Sunday
I should show respect to everyone including God, Christians, and government leaders (1 Peter 2:17).

Monday
God's holiness demands my respect at all times (Revelation 4:8-11).

Tuesday
God cares about my relationship with my parents. I need to obey them with respect (Exodus 20:12; Leviticus 19:3)

Wednesday
I need to respect the adults God put in my life who are working hard to help me grow into a woman of God (Leviticus 19:32; 1 Thessalonians 5:12-13).

Thursday
One of the ways I can show respect for my country's leaders is by praying for them each day (Ephesians 6:5; 1 Peter 2:17).

Friday
I must earn the respect of others with my daily words and actions (1 Thessalonians 4:11-12).

■ Something to Think About

How did you show respect to someone this week?

_____

_____

_____

Dear Jesus,

I praise you for _____

_____

_____

I'm sorry for _____

_____

_____

I ask you for _____

_____

_____

I thank you for _____

_____

_____ Amen.

Who Gains Respect?

Decode the puzzle to discover who gains respect (Proverbs 11:16a).

α   κ ι ν δ η ε α ρ τ ε δ   ω ο μ α ν   γ α ι ν σ

ρ ε σ π ε χ τ .

Key					
	A = α	G = γ	L = λ	Q = θ	V = ϖ
	B = β	H = η	M = μ	R = ρ	W = ω
	C = χ	I = ι	N = ν	S = σ	X = Ξ
	D = δ	J = φ	O = ο	T = τ	Y = ψ
	E = ε	K = κ	P = π	U = υ	Z = ζ
	F = φ				

■ Theme for the Week: Witnessing

■ Key Verse for thc Week

Therefore go and make disciples of all nations, baptizing them in the name of the Father and of the Son and of the Holy Spirit, and teaching them to obey everything I have commanded you. And surely I am with you always, to the very end of the age.
—Matthew 28:19-20

■ Bible Reading: Matthew 28:16-20

The Domino Effect

Have you ever taken a pile of dominoes and stood them up in a row, each behind the others? You push the first domino, which hits the next one, which bumps into its neighbor, and soon the whole line is lying flat. That's called the domino effect.

Towards the end of his time on earth, Jesus gathered his disciples around him and told them to make disciples of all the nations. The disciples obeyed Jesus' command— each disciple told someone about Jesus, and that person told the next person about Jesus, and then that person told her neighbor about Jesus. Telling people about Jesus is called witnessing. The way it works is something like the domino effect.

Jesus' command to the disciples—we call it the Great Commission—is your theme verse for the week. Read Matthew 28:19-20 one more time. Did you know that Jesus is talking to you too?

Witnessing didn't end with Jesus and his disciples in Galilee. When you believe in Jesus, you are his disciple too. And there are still people who need to hear the good news about Jesus and his love. Listen to his voice. He's calling you today.

■ Something to Think About

Who are you going to share the love of Jesus with today? Don't forget to pray for this person.

_____

Dear Jesus,

I praise you for _____
_____
_____

I'm sorry for _____
_____
_____

I ask you for _____
_____
_____

I thank you for _____
_____
_____ Amen.

Witnessing Maze

Help this disciple make her way to the person who needs to hear about Jesus' love.

START

■ Theme for the Week: Witnessing

■ Key Verse for the Week

Therefore go and make disciples of all nations, baptizing them in the name of the Father and of the Son and of the Holy Spirit, and teaching them to obey everything I have commanded you. And surely I am with you always, to the very end of the age.
—Matthew 28:19-20

■ Bible Reading: James 3:3-12

You Can't Have It Both Ways!

When I was eleven years old my family invited our pastor over one night. The pastor asked me and my brother and sisters questions from the Bible. I knew every answer! I used wonderful words when I told the pastor how much I loved Jesus. My mom and dad were very proud of me.

After the pastor left, my sister and I started to fight while we were washing and drying dishes. I called her some very mean names and told her that I wished she wasn't my sister. What horrible words I used!

My parents were disappointed. They said, "How can a girl say such nice things to the pastor and such terrible things to her sister?"

The Bible says the same thing in James 3:9-10. "With the tongue we praise our Lord and Father, and with it we curse men, who have been made in God's likeness. Out of the same mouth come praise and cursing. . . . This should not be." When it comes to witnessing, you can't have it both ways!

■ Something to Think About

How's your witness for Jesus? Are your words and actions praising Jesus or disappointing him? You can't have it both ways!

Dear Jesus,

I praise you for _____

_____

_____

I'm sorry for _____

_____

_____

I ask you for _____

_____

_____

I thank you for _____

_____

_____ Amen.

Grid Drawing

To be an effective witness your words *and* actions need to be the same—both must praise God! On the grid is half of a Bible. Draw the other half of the Bible and make it look the same. Then add your favorite Bible verse.

■ Theme for the Week: Witnessing

■ Key Verse for the Week

Therefore go and make disciples of all nations, baptizing them in the name of the Father and of the Son and of the Holy Spirit, and teaching them to obey everything I have commanded you. And surely I am with you always, to the very end of the age.
—*Matthew 28:19-20*

■ Bible Reading: 1 John 5:9-12

Tuck the Testimony in Your Heart!

Do you know someone who wears a locket on a necklace? Ask your grandma if she has one you can see. It's likely you'll find a tiny picture of someone she loves tucked inside. People wear lockets to remind them of loved ones and to keep them close to their hearts.

Even if you don't have a locket, today's Bible passage talks about something you need to tuck into your heart. Anybody who believes in Jesus, it says, has a testimony to keep in her heart. "And this is the testi-mony: God has given us eternal life, and this life is in his Son" (1 John 5:11).

Knowing and believing in Jesus as your Savior is a testimony you can treasure and keep tucked away in your heart forever. It's also a testimony that needs to be shared with the people around you.

When you open your grandma's locket and see a picture of your grandpa inside, you'll know that she loves him very much! And when you witness to other people about Jesus and share the testimony in your heart, they'll know that you love Jesus very much!

■ Something to Think About

Tucking Jesus' testimony in your heart is better than a gold or silver locket. Don't believe it? Read Job 22:25!

Dear Jesus,

I praise you for _____

_____

_____

I'm sorry for _____

_____

_____

I ask you for _____

_____

_____

I thank you for _____

_____

_____ Amen.

Heart Sandwich

What You Need
2 slices of bread
1 slice American or cheddar cheese

How to Do It
1. Toast the two slices of bread.
2. Place the cheese (tuck it!) between the pieces of toast.
3. Microwave the sandwich for 30 seconds or until cheese melts.
4. Cut the outer edges of the crust to form a heart.
5. Make extra heart sandwiches and share them with your family and friends. Tell them what you learned about the testimony that is in your heart.

■ Theme for the Week: Witnessing

■ Key Verse for the Week

Therefore go and make disciples of all nations, baptizing them in the name of the Father and of the Son and of the Holy Spirit, and teaching them to obey everything I have commanded you. And surely I am with you always, to the very end of the age.
—Matthew 28:19-20

■ Bible Reading: Isaiah 52:7

Beautiful Feet

When I was twelve years old I was constantly teased because of my large feet. One of the popular boys in my class told me I was just like the famous poet Longfellow. At first I thought he liked the story I had just finished writing for English class. But I realized the painful truth when he pointed at my feet and started laughing. He said, "Your feet are longfellows too!"

Maybe it's because of my big feet that I love Isaiah 52:7 so much: "How beautiful on the mountains are the feet of those who bring good news, who proclaim peace, who bring good tidings, who proclaim salvation, who say to Zion, 'Your God reigns!'"

It doesn't matter if you have large feet, small feet, or funny feet. It doesn't even matter if your legs and feet don't work the way most people's do.

What's important to God is that you tell others about Jesus. When you witness to others about Jesus' love, God says your feet are beautiful!

■ Something to Think About

Paint your toenails tonight (your favorite color!) and think about what really makes your feet beautiful to God! Praise God for giving you a heart full of love for Jesus.

Dear Jesus,

I praise you for _____

_____

_____

I'm sorry for _____

_____

_____

I ask you for _____

_____

_____

I thank you for _____

_____

_____ Amen.

Fancy Feet

What You Need

Old or new canvas shoes (Be sure to get your mom's permission for decorating them!)

Fabric paints

Ribbon

Beads

Hot glue gun

How to Do It

1. Plan your design on a sheet of paper before you begin. Be creative!
2. Make hearts, squiggles, flowers, or dot designs with the fabric paint.
3. Glue the beads on your shoes. Tie the ribbon into tiny bows and glue them on your shoes. Or use the ribbon for shoelaces!

■ Theme for the Week: Witnessing

■ Key Verse for the Week

Therefore go and make disciples of all nations, baptizing them in the name of the Father and of the Son and of the Holy Spirit, and teaching them to obey everything I have commanded you. And surely I am with you always, to the very end of the age.
—*Matthew 28:19-20*

■ Bible Reading: Matthew 5:14-16

How Bright Is Your Light?

Note: Have today's prayer and Bible reading time in a dark room. Use a flashlight or small lamp to give you enough light to read.

One of the best ways to witness to the people around you is by being a light. Many people don't know Jesus' love and forgiveness. Their lives are filled with sin and sadness. Turn your flashlight or small lamp off for a few minutes and think of some people you know who aren't Christians.

Now turn it back on again. The people you were thinking about need a light to show them the way to Jesus. When you witness to them and others, you are a shining light for him! Jesus says, "Let your light shine before men, that they may see your good deeds and praise your Father in heaven" (Matthew 5:16).

After you turned your light back on again, did you notice how it brightened the whole room? Be like your flashlight! Let your words and actions shine for Jesus in your home, school, church, and neighborhood. Go ahead and shine!

■ Something to Think About

Ask your dad or mom if you can eat your next evening meal by candlelight. Tell your family what you learned about shining for Jesus.

Dear Jesus,

I praise you for _____

_____

_____

I'm sorry for _____

_____

_____

I ask you for _____

_____

_____

I thank you for _____

_____

_____ Amen.

A Light Litany

Here is a litany you can use for family devotions this week. Let your light shine!

What You Need

A Bible for each member of the family

A candle in a holder for each person

Matches

How to Do It

1. Gather your family and friends into one room (if possible do this at night in a darkened room).
2. Ahead of time, look up the following verses and mark one or more in each Bible with a bookmark: Psalm 18:28; Psalm 119:105; John 8:12; Matthew 5:14-16; Romans 13:12; 1 John 1:5-7; 2 Corinthians 4:6; Ephesians 5:8-10.
3. Give each person a Bible (with the verse marked) and a candle.
4. Have the first person light his or her candle with a match and read the verse(s) marked in the Bible. The first person should then light the next person's candle with his or her candle. (Place the unlit candle in the flame of the lit candle.) Once the candle is lit, the second person may read a verse.
5. Continue reading and lighting candles until everyone has had a turn.
6. Finish by having someone close in prayer.

■ Theme for the Week: Witnessing

■ Key Verse for the Week

Therefore go and make disciples of all nations, baptizing them in the name of the Father and of the Son and of the Holy Spirit, and teaching them to obey everything I have commanded you. And surely I am with you always, to the very end of the age.
—Matthew 28:19-20

■ Bible Reading: 1 Peter 2:21-25

She's Copying Me!

Have you ever had someone copy everything you did? If you yawned, she would yawn. If you scratched your ear, she would scratch her ear. After awhile you probably got so irritated you complained to the nearest adult. "She's copying me! Make her stop!"

There is someone, though, who doesn't mind being copied all day long. In fact, nothing would make him happier than for you to copy his every step. Today's Bible passage says, "To this you were called, because Christ suffered for you, leaving you an example, that you should follow in his steps" (1 Peter 2:21).

Jesus wants you to copy the way he loves and forgives people. He wants you to copy his gentleness, patience, and kindness. He wants you to follow his prayer life and love for God's Word.

How's your witness? Are you imitating the way Jesus talked, acted, and prayed? Ask Jesus to help you follow in his steps today.

■ Something to Think About

Want to read more about following in Jesus' steps? Read *What Would Jesus Do?* by Mack Thomas (Multnomah). You'll find it in most church libraries and Christian bookstores.

Dear Jesus,

I praise you for _____

_____

_____

I'm sorry for _____

_____

_____

I ask you for _____

_____

_____

I thank you for _____

_____

_____ *Amen.*

Peanut Butter Treats

What You Need
1¼ cups (.30 L) dry milk powder
1¼ cups (.30 L) powdered sugar
1 cup (.24 L) peanut butter
1 cup (.24 L) corn syrup

How to Do It
1. Mix ingredients.
2. Take a small amount of mixture and make a small ball.
3. Try to copy the size and shape of the first ball with the rest of the mixture.
4. Share your treats with your family, friends, and neighbors. Tell them what you learned about copying Jesus.

■ Theme for the Week: Witnessing

■ Key Verse for the Week

Write the key verse for the week on the lines below.

_____

_____

_____

_____

_____

_____

—Matthew 28:19-20

■ This Week I Learned . . .

Sunday
The Great Commission Jesus gave his disciples is for me too. I need to tell others about Jesus (Matthew 28:16-20).

Monday
My words must be filled with praise for God, not meanness or anger towards others. As a witness for Jesus, I can't have it both ways (James 3:3-12).

Tuesday
When people see the testimony that's tucked into my heart, they'll know that I love Jesus very much! (1 John 5:9-12).

Wednesday
No matter how large, small, or funny my feet, God says they're beautiful if I witness for him (Isaiah 52:7).

Thursday
I need to let my words and actions shine for Jesus like a flashlight in a dark room (Matthew 5:14-16).

Friday
Jesus wants me to copy his life on earth! I'll be a witness for him if I follow in his steps (1 Peter 2:21-25).

■ Something to Think About

Who did you witness to this week? Write down how you showed this person that you love Jesus.

_____

_____

_____

Dear Jesus,

I praise you for _____

_____

_____

I'm sorry for _____

_____

_____

I ask you for _____

_____

_____

I thank you for _____

_____

_____ Amen.

Reflecting Jesus

What You Need
Hand mirror
Fabric or craft paint pens
    (your choice of colors)

How to Do It
1. Practice writing words with your paints on a piece of paper.
2. Lay your mirror on the table with the glass facing you.
3. Beginning in the top left-hand corner of the mirror, write the words "Reflecting Jesus!"
4. Along the sides and bottom of the glass, make small hearts or flowers.
5. Let the paint dry.
6. Every time you use your mirror, remember that you are a witness when your life reflects Jesus.

12

■ Theme for the Week: Servanthood

■ Key Verse for the Week

Love the LORD your God, . . . walk in all his ways, . . . obey his commands, . . . hold fast to him . . . and serve him with all your heart and all your soul.

—Joshua 22:5b

■ Bible Reading: Joshua 22:5

Heart and Soul Service

Living the life of a servant doesn't sound very glamorous. It's a lot more fun to be served than to serve, isn't it?

You might have the idea that being a servant involves aprons, mops, and dust rags. Maybe the word "servant" makes you think of Cinderella, who had to do all the cooking and cleaning for her cruel stepmother and wicked stepsisters.

That's nothing like God's idea of servanthood! Today's Bible passage tell us that God wants service to begin in the hearts and

souls of his people. "Serve him with all your heart and all your soul" (Joshua 22:5b). When your heart overflows with love for Jesus, it shows in your service to others.

God wants your heart and soul service. The more love you have for Jesus in your heart and soul, the more you'll want to serve him! With each new day, service will turn from a "must-do" job to a "want-to" privilege.

■ Something to Think About

List something that you're responsible for that you don't enjoy doing.

_____

Put your heart and soul into it today and turn it from a "must-do" to a "want-to" privilege.

Guess What, Jesus?

Dear Jesus,

I praise you for _____

_____

_____

I'm sorry for _____

_____

_____

I ask you for _____

_____

_____

I thank you for _____

_____

_____ Amen.

Servanthood Scripture

Change the numbers to letters and discover a message for servants.

A	B	C	D	E	F	G	H	I	J	K	L	M	N	O	P	Q	R	S	T	U	V	W	X	Y	Z
1	2	3	4	5	6	7	8	9	10	11	12	13	14	15	16	17	18	19	20	21	22	23	24	25	26

$\overline{19}\ \overline{5}\ \overline{18}\ \overline{22}\ \overline{5}$ $\overline{23}\ \overline{8}\ \overline{15}\ \overline{12}\ \overline{5}\ \overline{8}\ \overline{5}\ \overline{1}\ \overline{18}\ \overline{20}\ \overline{5}\ \overline{4}\ \overline{12}\ \overline{25}$,

$\overline{1}\ \overline{19}$ $\overline{9}\ \overline{6}$ $\overline{25}\ \overline{15}\ \overline{21}$ $\overline{23}\ \overline{5}\ \overline{18}\ \overline{5}$ $\overline{19}\ \overline{5}\ \overline{18}\ \overline{22}\ \overline{9}\ \overline{14}\ \overline{7}$

$\overline{20}\ \overline{8}\ \overline{5}$ $\overline{12}\ \overline{15}\ \overline{18}\ \overline{4}$, $\overline{14}\ \overline{15}\ \overline{20}$ $\overline{13}\ \overline{5}\ \overline{14}$.   (Ephesians 6:7)

■ Theme for the Week: Servanthood

■ Key Verse for the Week

Love the LORD your God, . . . walk in all his ways, . . . obey his commands, . . . hold fast to him . . . and serve him with all your heart and all your soul.

—*Joshua 22:5b*

■ Bible Reading: Matthew 20:26-28

Do You Want to Be Great?

What's the best way to be great when you're looking for a place to sit in your school's lunchroom?

_____ Look for the most popular girls in your class and sit with them.

_____ Sit by a girl who is lonely and has no one else sitting by her.

If you're only concerned with pleasing people, the best way to be great would be the first choice. But if you want to serve Jesus, searching for someone who needs a friend is the only choice.

Jesus' heavenly view of the lunchroom is just the opposite of our view. Matthew 20:26b-28a says, "Whoever wants to become great among you must be your servant, and whoever wants to be first must be your slave—just as the Son of Man did not come to be served, but to serve."

Jesus never promised that being a servant would be easy. He took his role as a servant so seriously that he died for you. Compared to Jesus' sacrifice and servanthood—from the manger to the cross to heaven—choosing to sit with a lonely girl doesn't seem so difficult, does it?

■ Something to Think About

Take your servanthood seriously. Don't just be a servant—be a *great* servant for the kingdom of heaven!

Dear Jesus,

I praise you for _____

_____

_____

I'm sorry for _____

_____

_____

I ask you for _____

_____

_____

I thank you for _____

_____

_____ Amen.

Friends and Family Book

One of the ways you can be a servant is by telling your friends and family how much you care for them. Keep their telephone numbers and e-mail addresses organized with a Friends and Family book.

What You Need

3" x 5" notecards (or plain paper)
Markers or a pen
Paper punch
Ribbon or string

How to Do It

1. Use one notecard per person. Write his or her name, e-mail address, and phone number on the card.
2. Punch two holes on the top of each notecard (make sure the holes on each card match).
3. Organize the cards in alphabetical order and tie them together with a string or ribbon.

■ **Theme for the Week:
Servanthood**

■ **Key Verse for the Week**

*Love the LORD your God, . . . walk in all his
ways, . . . obey his commands, . . . hold fast
to him . . . and serve him with all your heart
and all your soul.*

—*Joshua 22:5b*

■ **Bible Reading: Ephesians 6:7;
Philippians 2:14**

Whole♥ed Service

When your mom wakes you up on a
Saturday morning and says it's time to clean
your room and the garage, how do you
respond?

_____ Complain that your family never does
anything fun.

_____ Halfheartedly mumble, "OK. But it
better not take all day."

_____ Jump out of bed and say, "Where do
I start?"

If you were honest, you probably didn't
check the third option, right? When it comes
to service, complaining and halfhearted
mumbles roll easily from the tongues of
kids (and even adults!). It's difficult to be
enthusiastic about a day full of work, especially when you're still sleepy.

But being a sleepy servant doesn't change
the Bible's message about complaining and
service: "Do everything without complaining
or arguing" (Philippians 2:14). "Everything"
includes washing dishes, hanging up
clothes, and even sweeping the garage!

So next time somebody asks you to do
something for them, think of Ephesians 6:7:
"Serve wholeheartedly, as if you were serving the Lord, not men." And ask God to
help you turn your halfhearted mumbles
into wholehearted service for him.

■ **Something to Think About**

Do a ♥ check. Are you serving the Lord
wholeheartedly?

Dear Jesus,

I praise you for _____

_____

_____

I'm sorry for _____

_____

_____

I ask you for _____

_____

_____

I thank you for _____

_____

_____ Amen.

Heart Treats

What You Need
1¼ cups (.30 L) boiling water
2 packages (3 oz. or 84 g each) gelatin (pick your favorite flavor!)
8" x 8" square pan
Spatula

How to Do It
1. Ask an adult for permission to work in the kitchen.
2. Stir the boiling water and gelatin in a large bowl until the gelatin is dissolved (about 3 minutes).
3. Pour the mixture into pan.
4. Refrigerate at least 3 hours or until firm.
5. Dip the bottom of the pan in warm water for about 10 seconds (to make it easier to get the gelatin out of the pan).
6. Cut the gelatin with a heart-shaped cookie cutter.
7. Lift the hearts from the pan with a spatula.

12

■ **Theme for the Week: Servanthood**

■ **Key Verse for the Week**

Love the LORD your God, . . . walk in all his ways, . . . obey his commands, . . . hold fast to him . . . and serve him with all your heart and all your soul.

—*Joshua 22:5b*

■ **Bible Reading: Matthew 6:19-24**

Take Your Pick

Did you know that you need to choose between who or what to serve? According to today's Bible reading, you have to take your pick between serving God or serving money.

When you serve God, your focus is on people. Servanthood involves obeying your parents, caring for your classmates, and helping your neighbors. When you choose to serve, you're storing up treasures in heaven.

Serving money is the choice you make when *things* come first in your heart. Your treasure is right here on earth if your words and thoughts are filled with what name-brand clothes you wear, what CDs you own, and how much allowance you get each week.

Today's Bible passage says, "No one can serve two masters. Either he will hate the one and love the other, or he will be devoted to the one and despise the other. You cannot serve both God and Money" (Matthew 6:24). Who are you serving? Is it money, the things on earth that don't last? Or is it God, whose love for you will last an eternity?

■ **Something to Think About**

If you're not sure who or what you're serving, make a list of what's most important to you. What are your thoughts, words, and actions focused on most during the day?

Dear Jesus,

I praise you for _____

_____

_____

I'm sorry for _____

_____

_____

I ask you for _____

_____

_____

I thank you for _____

_____

_____ Amen.

Occupation Word Search

Find the following words that describe the kinds of jobs people have that serve people.

BEAUTICIAN
BUS DRIVER
DENTIST
NURSE
PASTOR
TEACHER
WAITRESS

R	T	E	A	C	H	E	R	T	B
O	E	N	U	R	S	E	X	E	D
T	C	V	I	X	X	T	A	S	E
R	J	Z	I	J	J	U	I	R	N
O	A	Z	W	R	T	C	N	U	T
T	J	B	T	I	D	C	W	O	I
S	J	A	C	S	A	S	O	O	S
A	C	I	Q	T	U	G	U	W	T
P	A	Y	C	Z	R	D	A	B	L
N	W	A	I	T	R	E	S	S	H

12

■ **Theme for the Week:
Servanthood**

■ **Key Verse for the Week**

*Love the LORD your God, . . . walk in all his
ways, . . . obey his commands, . . . hold fast
to him . . . and serve him with all your heart
and all your soul.*

—*Joshua 22:5b*

■ **Bible Reading: Romans 12:9-12**

Service with a Smile

Think of three things that make you smile
(things like playing volleyball with your
friends, eating a hot fudge sundae, or going
on a walk with your dad).

_____

_____

_____

You laugh and smile a lot when you're
doing things that you enjoy. It's easy for
others to see that you're happy. Do you
serve the Lord with the same enthusiasm as
when you're doing the things you listed? Is
there joy in your face and in your heart
when you're serving Jesus?

Romans 12:11-12 is brimming with action-
packed advice on how to give the Lord
your service with a smile.

- Never be lacking in *zeal.* (Be passion-
  ate about your faith!)
- Keep your spiritual *fervor.* (Be persistent in telling others about Jesus!)
- Be *joyful* in hope. (Be cheerful! You've
  been promised an eternity on the gold-
  en streets of heaven! See Revelation
  21:21.)

Remember, you can be a super servant for
the Lord through your zeal, fervor, joy—and
yes, your sweet smile!

■ **Something to Think About**

Make it your goal to have at least three
people ask you today, "What are you smiling about?" Then tell them why!

Dear Jesus,

I praise you for _____

_____

_____

I'm sorry for _____

_____

_____

I ask you for _____

_____

_____

I thank you for _____

_____

_____ Amen.

Smile Treats

What You Need
Apple
Miniature marshmallows
Peanut butter

How to Do It
1. Ask an adult for permission to work in the kitchen.
2. Cut apple into eight slices. Remove seeds.
3. Spread peanut butter on one side of each slice.
4. Top four of the slices with miniature marshmallows. Line them up like a row of teeth.
5. Put the remaining four slices on top of each row of teeth.
6. Share your Smile Treats with others and tell them what you learned about serving the Lord with a smile.

—Adapted from *Caterpillar Scramble and Cantaloupe Boats* by Noreen Thomas, RR1 Box 173, Moorhead MN 56560. Doubting Thomas Publishing Co., 1997. Used by permission.

■ **Theme for the Week:
Servanthood**

■ **Key Verse for the Week**

*Love the LORD your God, . . . walk in all his
ways, . . . obey his commands, . . . hold fast
to him . . . and serve him with all your heart
and all your soul.*

—*Joshua 22:5b*

■ **Bible Reading: 1 Peter 4:10-11**

To God Be the Glory!

God gives each of his children special talents that they can use to serve Jesus. Maybe
you're a wonderful artist who can make
beautiful get-well cards. Maybe you love
little kids, and you sometimes help the busy
mom next door by looking after her little
ones. Or maybe you're super-organized, and
you keep your family and friends on track!

Whenever you use your talents to the best
of your ability, people probably give you
compliments. They say things like, "Good
job! You're great at that! Keep it up!"

It feels great to be complimented! And it's
nice to have people appreciate the service
you do for them. The one danger in getting
lots of compliments is that you might want
to serve others only so you'll receive their
thanks and praise.

Today's Bible passage says, "If anyone
serves, he should do it with the strength
God provides, so that in all things God may
be praised through Jesus Christ. To him be
the glory and the power for ever and ever.
Amen" (1 Peter 4:11).

That means you should always use the gifts
God gave you for God's service—and his
glory. So the next time someone gives you
a compliment, smile and enjoy it. And give
God the glory!

■ **Something to Think About**

What are some of the talents God has given
you? Think about how you can use them to
serve others and bring praise and honor to
God's name.

Dear Jesus,

I praise you for _____
_____
_____

I'm sorry for _____
_____
_____

I ask you for _____
_____
_____

I thank you for _____
_____
_____ Amen.

Match the Talents

Match the person to the talent that God gave them. To check your answers, look up the passages.

Dorcas   Business woman who sold purple cloth (Acts 16:14)

Solomon   Mighty hunter (Genesis 10:9)

Lydia   Best neighbor (Luke 10:30-37)

Good Samaritan   Wise king (2 Chronicles 1:11-12)

Nimrod   Seamstress (Acts 9:39)

■ Theme for the Week: Servanthood

■ Key Verse for the Week

Write the key verse for the week on the lines below.

_____

_____

_____

_____

—*Joshua 22:5b*

■ This Week I Learned . . .

Sunday
Serving others is a privilege. I can show my love for Jesus through my heart and soul service (Joshua 22:5).

Monday
Jesus' view of being great is completely opposite of the world's view. If I want to be great in God's kingdom, I need to be a servant! (Matthew 20:26-28).

Tuesday
Servants should not complain about their work. I should serve wholeheartedly (Ephesians 6:7, Philippians 2:14).

Wednesday
I must choose what or who I will serve: the things of this world or God, whose love lasts for an eternity (Matthew 6:19-24).

Thursday
Being a super servant for the Lord means I'll give service with a smile—with zeal, fervor, and joy (Romans 12:9-12).

Friday
God gave me special talents to help me serve him and bring praise and glory to God's name (1 Peter 4:10-11).

■ Something to Think About

How did you serve the Lord this week?

_____

_____

_____

Dear Jesus,

I praise you for _____

_____

_____

I'm sorry for _____

_____

_____

I ask you for _____

_____

_____

I thank you for _____

_____

_____ Amen.

Balloon Fun

Do you know someone who could use an extra smile today? Be a servant and share some smiles with these fun balloons.

What You Need
Balloons
Markers

How to Do It
1. Use your markers to draw a picture on a balloon (hearts, smiley faces, or your own idea) when there's no air in it. You can also personalize the balloon by writing your friend's name or a cheerful message!
2. After the balloon is dry, surprise your friend by mailing her the special balloon.

For your privacy we have given you a cover that closes. Simply fold the back cover over the front, and insert the tab into the slot on the front cover.

① FOLD IN COVER

② FOLD TAB INTO SLOT

guess what, Jesus?